Essential Communication Skills

Essential Communication Skills

Shalini Aggarwal
Senior Lecturer, in Business Communication
NDIM, New Delhi

Ane Books Pvt. Ltd.
New Delhi ♦ Chennai

Essential Communication Skills

Shalini Aggarwal

First Edition : 2009

Reprint : 2009, 2011, 2013, 2016, 2017, 2018, **2020**

Published by

Ane Books Pvt. Ltd.

4821, Parwana Bhawan, 1st Floor, 24 Ansari Road, Darya Ganj,
New Delhi - 110 002, Tel.: +91(011) 23276843-44, Fax: +91(011) 23276863
e-mail: kapoor@anebooks.com, Website: www.anebooks.com

Branch Office:

- Avantika Niwas, 1st Floor, 19 Doraiswamy Road, T. Nagar,
  Chennai - 600 017, Tel.: +91(044) 28141554, 28141209
  e-mail: anebookschennai@gmail.com, rathinam@anebooks.com

ISBN : 978-81-8052-280-2

Preface

When a baby sees its mother's face for the first time, communication happens. When two strangers are sitting together without uttering a single word, communication is happening. When a computer in Delhi calls up a computer in Singapore and transmits a message, communication happens.

Communication is a general phenomenon. It occurs everywhere. Whether we admit it or not, we have no choice but to communicate. Sometimes we try to avoid communication by not replying to messages, hardly do we realize that we are still sending a message

The only choice we can make about communication is whether we are going to attempt to **communicate effectively**.

Your first job requires you to communicate effectively. You will read information, you will listen to instructions, and you will ask questions, you may solve problems with other workers in teams.

Organizations completely understand that achieving success in today's workplace is closely tied to the ability of managers to communicate effectively with each other and with people outside the organization. **Communication** is the process of sending and receiving messages. However, communication is **effective** only when the message is understood and when it stimulates action or encourages the receiver to think in new ways.

Your ability to **communicate effectively** increases productivity, both yours and your organization's. With good communication skills, you can anticipate problems, make decisions, coordinate work flow, supervise others, develop relationships, and promote products and services. You can shape the impressions you and your company makes on colleagues, employees, supervisors, investors and customers.

Without effective communication, people misunderstand each other and misinterpret information.

Effective communication skills: building critical skills helps you build and enhance your communication skills that are crucial for success in the 21st century workplace.

Author

Preface

Acknowledgement

My thanks are due to a great many people, who have, in various ways, helped in the preparation of this Book : to my parents and my sister, who were a constant source of advice and encouragement throughout the time of my attempting to write this book. I am really grateful to my maternal uncle and aunt for always believing in me inspiring me to go for higher education.

I have a real debt of gratitude to Prof. S.S. Sharma, Director, Netaji Subhash Institute of Management Sciences (NIMS), New Delhi for showing the light to me and carving my professional life.

In the end, but most importantly, I would like to thank Mr. J.R. Kapoor, Ane Books Pvt. Ltd. for giving me the opportunity to reach out to a wider audience.

Contents

Chapter

1

Basics of Communication

Learning Objectives

- Understanding the concept of business communication
- Getting familiar with the communication process
- Learning the importance of communication in today's world
- Understanding the seven C's of communication
- Learning about the channels of communication

Communication is not only the essence of being human, but also a vital property of life.

—***John A. Piece***

INTRODUCING BUSINESS COMMUNICATION

When a baby sees its mother's face for the first time, communication happens. When two strangers are sitting together without uttering a single word, communication happens. When a computer in Delhi transmits a message to a computer in Singapore, communication happens.

Communication is a general phenomenon. It occurs everywhere. Whether we admit it or not, we have no choice but to communicate. Sometimes we try to avoid communication by not replying to messages; hardly do we realise that we are still sending a message, but it may not be the one we want or intend. The only choice we can make about communication is whether we wish to make an attempt to communicate effectively.

Communication means to convey the thoughts, intentions, emotions, facts and opinions of one person or group to others. When the message sent is received and understood by the receiver in the same sense as the sender intended to convey, effective communication takes place.

Though business communication is a specialised branch of general communication, there is no basic difference between the two. The process is the same and so are the principles that regulate it. The difference lies in their application to situations. Whereas general communication plays diverse roles, business communication is specifically concerned with well-defined business activities.

An organisation is a group of persons constituted to achieve certain specific objectives. The achievement of these objectives or goals depends upon proper coordination of human effort in the organisation. The people working in the organisation are interrelated; their activities are also interrelated because they perform to achieve common organisational goals – which are possible only if there is an effective system of communication in the organisation.

COMMUNICATION PROCESS

Communication is a process that involves certain distinct steps. Communication is not complete till the message conveyed by the sender is properly understood by the receiver. Any communication process should necessarily have the following elements :

1. **Sender (Encoder):** The communication process begins with the sender who wishes to send a message to the receiver. The sender is also called the 'encoder' because 'to encode' is to put a message into words or images.

2. **Message:** The message is what the sender wants to convey to the receiver. It can be an idea, feeling, or a piece of information. In business communication, every message has a purpose or objective. The sender wishes – consciously or unconsciously – to accomplish something by communicating.
3. **Medium or Channel:** It is the medium of transmission from one person to another and is often inseparable from the message. For communication to be efficient and effective, the channel must be appropriate for the message. However, one does not always have an option of choosing the mode of communication. One must make individual decisions for each situation.
4. **Receiver (Decoder):** Receiver is the person or group for whom the communication is intended. If the message does not reach the receiver, communication has not happened. Receiver decodes the message thereby interpreting and translating it into meaningful information. Hence, a receiver is also known as a 'decoder'.
5. **Feedback:** It is the reaction to receiving the message. Without it the sender cannot know whether the receiver has received or grasped the message or not. Feedback is the return of a portion of the message to the sender with new information. The greater the feedback, the more effective the communication has been.
6. **Noise:** Noise is any disturbance that reduces, obscures, or disrupts the clarity or the quality of the message being transmitted. In other words, it is any interference that takes place between the sender and the receiver. That is why any communication problem which cannot be fully explained is called 'noise'.

The whole process is straightforward—the sender encodes the message and transmits it through the most appropriate channel to the receiver who decodes it and sends the corresponding feedback.

IMPORTANCE OF COMMUNICATION IN TODAY'S WORLD

The importance of communication has increased manifold with the passage of time as society is becoming more and more complex and businesses global. If you can communicate effectively, you have a high valued skill. Listed below are some of the benefits of effective communication :

- **Lifeblood of every organisation:** An organisation is a group of people associated for business, political, professional, religious, and social or other purposes. It cannot function without open and effective communication. Its activities require human beings to interact and react, that is to communicate.

- **Global business environment:** When dealing with people of different cultures and languages, there is need for effective communication.
- **Large scale operations:** With expansion, size and decentralisation of the organisation increases. Coordinating the whole affair needs effective communication.
- **Technological advancement:** With upcoming technologies paving the way every day, communicating to people through these modern technologies is very important.
- **Change in management style:** In today's scenario, the focus has shifted from all-powerful management to participative management. For it to succeed, effective communication styles are needed.
- **To the customer, you are the company:** Your attitude when dealing with customers, clients and the public reflect the company you represent. When dealing with international business people, your attitude will reflect your country and culture. Therefore, your ability to communicate orally and in writing affects your company's public image.
- **Need for better human relations:** To keep people motivated is an important task of management which calls for the need for effective communication skills.
- **Increasing social roles** in modern businesses.

SEVEN C'S OF COMMUNICATION

To compose effective written or oral messages, application of certain communication principles is necessary. These principles provide guidelines for choice of content and style of presentation, adapted to the purpose and the receiver of the message.

They are called the seven C's :

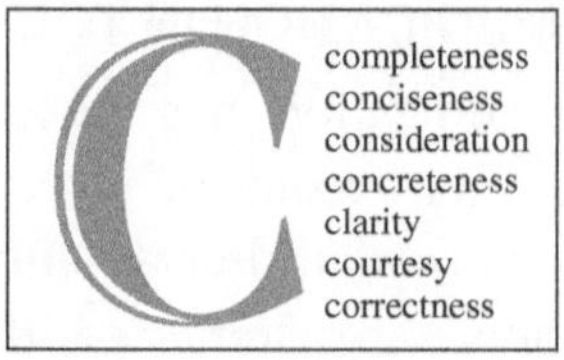

They are applicable to all forms of communication – be it mere expressions and sentences to complete documents and presentations.

1. **Completeness:** The business message is complete when it contains all facts that the reader or listener needs. Senders need to assess their messages through the eyes of receivers to be sure that they have included all the relevant information.

   Completeness has numerous benefits. Firstly, complete messages are more likely to bring the desired results without the expense of additional messages. Secondly, complete messages build goodwill and show concern for others. Thirdly, complete messages can avert lawsuits that may result if important information is missing.

   Remember to provide all necessary information. Answering the five W's helps make the message complete: who, what, when, where, and why.

   - Try to answer all questions – stated or implied. An incomplete reply may indicate carelessness or purposeful intentions to conceal a weak spot.
   - Give something extra, 'when desirable'. For example, you receive an inquiry from an out-of-town client regarding a particular club in your city. Realising that the client is new to the city, apart from the name of the club and its address, you can also furnish details like directions for reaching the club, facilities provided, landmarks, etc. Your message will then have that 'something extra' which the reader needs and will appreciate.

2. **Conciseness:** Conciseness is conveying the message in fewest possible words. A concise message is complete without being too wordy. This principle is very important in effective business communication because it saves time and expense for both sender and receiver. By eliminating unnecessary words, important ideas are made to stand out. It also shows respect for the recipient by not cluttering his/her professional life with unnecessary information.

   - Eliminate wordy expressions. Use single word substitutes instead of phrases, whenever possible, without changing meanings. For example,

     At this time – Now

     In due course – Soon

     Due to the fact that – Because

     - Include only relevant material and stick to the purpose of the message. Try to omit information obvious to the receiver; also avoid long introductions and unnecessary explanations.

- Avoid unnecessary repetitions as they lead to dullness. Use pronouns and initials instead of repeating long names.

3. **Consideration:** It implies preparing every message with the receiver in mind by trying to put yourself in their place. This is known as 'you attitude' – also called empathy, human touch, or understanding of human nature. A person preparing a 'you' message is aware of the receiver's desires, problems, circumstances, emotions and probable reactions.
   - Show audience benefit or interest in the receiver. Benefits must meet the recipients' needs, address their concerns, or offer them rewards.
   - Another way of showing consideration is to emphasise positive, pleasant facts. This means stressing on what can be done rather than what cannot be done, and focusing on favourable words for your recipient.
4. **Concreteness:** Communicating concretely means being specific, definite, and vivid rather than vague and general. It involves using denotative words rather than connotative ones.

   A **denotation** is usually the dictionary definition of a word, provided that the communicators are using the same language and have similar understanding of the context in which the word is used. They do not indicate any positive or negative qualities. For example, car, house, desk, book, etc.

   On the other hand, a **connotation** is an implied meaning of a word or a suggestion separate from the definition. It arouses qualitative judgments and personal reactions. For example, the term house is denotative. The connotations would be villa, mansion, cottage, shack, etc. Similarly, the word student is denotative; bookworm, scholar is connotative. The connotative meaning for words is affected by the communicators' varied backgrounds and interests.

   To communicate effectively, ensure that the receiver is aware of the connotative meanings of the words. Thus, choose the language carefully and consider both its denotations and connotations to convey the exact and concrete idea to achieve desired results.

Remember,

- Use specific facts and figures.
- Choose vivid, image building words. Business writing uses less figurative language.

5. **Clarity:** Conveying the meaning from the sender to the receiver – accurately – is the purpose of clarity. This is not easy because everybody has their own interpretations, ideas, experiences associated with words. Clarity is achieved in part through a balance between precise language and familiar language.
   - Choose precise, concrete and familiar words. Whenever you have a choice between a long word and a short one, use the short, familiar word that the recipient will quickly understand.
   - Construct effective sentences and paragraphs. Generally, short sentences are preferred. Unity and coherence are the key points to be kept in mind while constructing grammatically right sentences. It is also important to lay proper 'emphasis' on parts of sentences and paragraphs. Try to put the main ideas upfront within a sentence.
6. **Courtesy:** Courtesy involves being aware of the feelings of others. It comes from a sincere 'you-attitude'. It is not mere politeness, but something that grows out of respect and concern for others.
   - Be thoughtful and appreciative.
   - Use expressions that show respect. No reader wants to receive messages that offend.
   - Always omit questionable humour. What is laughable to one person may be disgusting for another–each one of us has a different sense of humour.
   - Choose non-discriminatory expressions – that is, equal treatment of people regardless of their gender, race, ethnic origin, and physical features.
7. **Correctness:** It involves use of proper grammar, punctuation and spelling. However, a message may be perfect grammatically, but still insult and thus lose a client. Keep in mind the following points :
   - Use the right level of language. There are three levels of language: formal writing is often associated with scholarly writing – thesis, dissertations, legal documents, agreements,

etc. The style is not conversational but impersonal and contains long sentences.

Informal writing is more characteristic of business writing. Here, the words are short, conversational and slightly familiar.

Substandard language which refers to use of incorrect words, incorrect grammar, slang, indicating an inability to use good English, should be completely avoided.

- Check accuracy of figures, facts and words.

CHANNELS OF COMMUNICATION

A channel of communication is the path through which information flows throughout the organisation. It may be formal or informal.

Formal Channels

These are the systems designed by the management to dictate who should talk to whom to get a job done. This network is created to regulate the flows of communication so as to avoid any confusion and make everything more orderly, timely and smooth. All upward, downward and horizontal communications flow through this network.

- **Downward communication:** It occurs when messages flow from top management through various levels to the bottom of the organisation. There may be several types of messages.
  - Job procedures / instructions. Directions about what to do and how to do
  - Explanation of policies and practices
  - Giving feedback to subordinates and motivating them.

  This communication helps the subordinates to know what is expected of them and brings in greater job satisfaction.
- **Upward communication:** It involves messages flowing from subordinates to superiors. Upward communication is important because it helps the top management in knowing about the attitudes, behaviour, opinions, activities and feelings of the workers on the job. Subordinates also get an outlet to air their grievances, suggestions and opinions etc. They may also feel that they are contributing towards the goals of the organisation.
- **Horizontal and lateral communication:** This is between persons of the same hierarchical level; it may be between members of the same division of an organisation. It helps in coordinating the activities of different departments at the same level.

- **Diagonal or crosswise communication:** It cuts across functions and levels in an organisation. When a supervisor in the credit department communicates directly with the regional marketing manager, who is not only in a different department but also at a higher level, it is known as diagonal communication.

Informal Channels

These channels are formed to meet needs that are not satisfied by formal communication. Employees form friendships, they talk in gatherings and fill in communication gaps within the formal channels. Such channels are not authentic and the message may get distorted. The responsibility of the communicator also cannot be fixed as the communication is oral in nature. But the advantages are that it satisfies social needs and fosters better human relations. It is a very speedy network to spread the information. Some of the sources are :

- Social gatherings
- When managers informally walk through the work area and casually talk to employees.
- **Grapevine:** The channel mostly associated with gossips and rumors. It is the most widespread and commonly used network. The grapevine exists outside the formal channels and is the expression of natural motivation to communicate.

Characteristics of Grapevine

1. Grapevine emerges from the social and personal interaction of the employees.
2. The transmission flows in all directions in the organisation.
3. Most grapevine communication is oral.
4. It is a speedy network.
5. It can end anywhere in the organisation – spatially as well as hierarchically.
6. As the size of the organisation increases, grapevine activity increases.

Patterns of Grapevine

1. **The single strand:** It is the way in which most people view the grapevine. In this, *A* tells something to *B*, *B* further tells it to *C*, who tells it to another and so forth. This chain is least accurate in passing the information.
2. **Gossip chain:** In this, one person seeks out and tells everyone the information that he has obtained.

3. **Probability chain:** Here the individuals are indifferent about whom they offer information to. They tell people at random and those people in turn tell others at random.
4. **Cluster chain:** In this, person *A* conveys the information to a few selected individuals; some of these individuals then inform a few selected others. It is believed that the cluster chain is the most popular pattern that grapevine communications take.

POINTS TO REMEMBER

- Communication means conveying the thoughts, intentions, ideas, opinions, and facts of one person or group to others.
- The communication process is straightforward: the sender encodes the message and transmits it through the most appropriate channel to the receiver who decodes it and sends the corresponding feedback.
- The importance of communication has all the more increased with the passage of time as society is becoming more and more complex and businesses global.
- Certain communication principles are necessary: Seven C's – completeness, conciseness, consideration, concreteness, clarity, courtesy, and correctness.
- A channel of communication is the path through which information flows throughout the organisation. It may be formal or informal.
- Grapevine (informal communication network) is the most widespread and commonly used network.

Chapter

2

Types of Communication

Learning Objectives

- Understanding the different types of communication – verbal and non-verbal
- Knowing the nature of verbal communication – oral and written
- Knowing the nature and different types of non-verbal communicat-ion
- Learning about different types of non-verbal communication – body language, sign language, paralanguage, circumstantial language
- Learning that appearance is an important factor in communication

Communication leads to community, that is, to understanding, intimacy and mutual valuing.

—Rollo May

Broadly classified, communication can be divided into two categories :

1. Verbal communication
2. Non-verbal communication

VERBAL COMMUNICATION

The term 'verbal' denotes the use of words. When words are used in communication – be it spoken or written it is termed as verbal communication.

Oral Communication

It is communication by way of uttering words, *i.e.*, speaking. Speaking is the fastest, most direct type of communication. Every time we speak, our voice reveals our gender, age, geographic background, level of education, emotional state and the relationship with the person spoken to. Oral communication can be of various forms in an organisation – meetings, conferences, face to face communication, telephone calls, et al.

Advantages

- It is a speedy and fast way of communication.
- The speaker is able to get the personal attention of the receiver.
- It allows instant feedback.
- Confidentiality is assured as no records are created.
- It is supplemented by non-verbal signals.

Disadvantages

- It is not suitable in complex and controversial messages.
- It is expensive and time consuming when distant locations are involved.
- It leaves no documentary proof.
- It is more prone to physical noise.

Written Communication

Preparing written messages is of paramount importance in all spheres of life. These can be of various types – memorandums, business letters, fax messages, reports, notices and proposals. To be effective, written communication must be clear, complete, correct and understandable.

Advantages

- It is permanent and can be used for future reference.
- It can be composed in advance and so is less prone to errors.
- It can address more number of persons at a time.

- It leaves more lasting impact because it is visual.
- It is less prone to physical noise.

Disadvantages

- It is time consuming.
- Certain messages cannot be put in writing.
- Interpretation may vary.
- Immediate feedback is not possible.
- It is not possible to see non-verbal signs.
- It lacks of confidentiality as written messages can pass through several hands.

NON-VERBAL COMMUNICATION

Non-verbal communication involves neither written nor spoken words. Most of us spend about 75 per cent of our waking hours communicating our knowledge, thoughts and ideas to others. However, most of us fail to realise that a great deal of our communication is in a non-verbal form as opposed to the oral and written forms. Non-verbal communication includes facial expressions, eye contact, tone of voice, body posture and motions, and positioning within groups. It may also include the way one wears clothes or remains silent.

Recall a conversation during which you raised your eyebrows to convey your disbelief at a statement made by your partner, or a meeting in which you appreciated a member by patting his / her back. Remember that deafening roar of applause that you received at the end of an inaugural address delivered by you to a large audience in the huge conference hall of an organisation.

All the situations mentioned above convey a significant fact – we communicate not only through words but also through means other than words.

There are different types of non-verbal communication as given below :

- Body language
- Sign language
- Paralanguage
- Circumstantial language

BODY LANGUAGE (KINESICS)

Body language is the communication of personal feelings, emotions, attitudes and thoughts through body movements, gestures, postures, facial expressions, walking styles, positions and other demeanours, either consciously or unconsciously, whether accompanied or not accompanied by verbal communication. In simple words, it is the way the body communicates by its physical movements.

Facial Expressions

The human face is the most complex and versatile among all species, serving many different functions. It serves as a window to display one's own state of mind. Your boss's smile makes you feel happy while his frown leaves you uncomfortable; your subordinate's confused expression tells you to continue with the explanation; your customer's smile and nodding signal indicates that it is time to close the sale.

Thus, facial expressions can divulge hidden emotions – anger, annoyance, confusion, enthusiasm, fear, hatred, joy, love, interest, agony, sorrow, surprise, uncertainty and others. While in conversation, a smile shows that the interaction has been pleasant for both the parties. Even in a telephonic conversation, one is able to feel the impact of a smiling voice.

However, facial expressions, like other non-verbal signs, may be ambiguous at times.

Eye Movements

Facial expressions, especially eyes, draw immediate attention to the unstated part of the message that goes with words to communicate the total meaning of what is being conveyed. Eyes tell us much more than other facial features. While communicating, remember the popular saying – face reflects the mind; eyes reflect the heart.

For example, eye contact shows attentiveness. Partly closed eyes indicate reflectiveness. Rolling eyes indicate restlessness as if they are looking for something more. Staring eyes communicate threat. Wide open eyes show wonder or shock. A wink, following a statement contradicts the seriousness of the statement made. Raised eyebrows or wrinkled forehead is associated with objection and questioning. Avoiding eye contact shows nervousness, or trying to conceal something.

The point to note is that one must not over-generalise because people differ and there are exceptions on individual non-verbal cues.

Posture

It is the way we carry ourselves. One may choose to stand or sit erect, or lean forward or backward, or slouch haphazardly. Postures non-verbally convey impressions of self-confidence, status and interest. Interested persons normally lean forward towards the speaker, while those who are bored or annoyed may slouch and yawn and repeatedly glance at their watches. The way one sits at the workstation when one is working indicates their attitude towards the job.

The posture tells whether a person is tense or relaxed. Body tension or relaxation is a strong indicator of who has the power in one to one relationships. As a rule, the more relaxed person in a given situation has the greater status.

A list of some postures and the message they communicate is given below :

- Slumped posture: low spirits
- Erect posture: high spirits, energy and confidence
- Lean forward: open and interested
- Lean away: defensive or not interested
- Crossed arms: defensive
- Uncrossed arms: willingness to listen

Gestures

They are the physical movements of arms, legs, hands, torso and head. Although gestures are spontaneous, one can learn to monitor and use the positive gestures and minimise the negative ones. Positive gestures are body signals which make you look relaxed, confident and polite.

Positive Gestures

- Good listening gestures include leaning a little towards the speaker, eye contact, and nodding the head as a sign of agreement with what is said.
- Good speaking gestures include keeping your hands open. Avoid clutching them or folding them across the chest as it reflects a closed mind.
- Avoid putting both your hands in pockets. If you put one hand in your pocket, it shows arrogance, if you put both, it shows nervousness.
- Impressive moving gestures involve walking with your head upright. Hands should swing freely on your sides. Eyes should look straight in front.
- The proper way of carrying books, files and documents is to carry them on one side, rather than clutching them against the chest.

Negative Gestures

- *Nervousness*: Hands in pockets, scratching your head, biting nails, covering the mouth while speaking, glancing sideways, speaking too fast or slow, drumming fingers, sitting on the edge of the chair, clearing your throat too often, tapping your foot, looking at the ceiling, crossing arms or legs, rocking your legs, straightening the tie, blinking a lot, playing with jewellery, watches or cufflinks, clicking pens, playing with paper weight, frequently sipping or drinking water, adjusting your glasses up the nose and setting the hair with hands too often are all nervous gestures.

- *Lack of etiquette/manners*: Banging the table instead of laughing at a joke, wiping hands across the face, chewing pens, waving hands around you when talking, opening or closing buttons, or setting your watch strap as you talk, and touching the nose time and again indicate a lack of etiquette/manners.
- *Aggressiveness*: Staring, pointing at someone, folding both arms, showing a fist, and bending over someone are signs of aggression.
- *Self-importance*: Eyes closed while talking, pursed mouth, head bent backwards while talking, looking at the tip of the nose while talking, looking over the top of glasses, waving glasses or key rings while talking all indicate that the person thinks too much of himself/herself.
- *Rudeness*: Shaking hands too hard or giving a limp handshake, looking at your watch during conversation, whispering at a social gathering, continuing to work while somebody is talking to you, yawning, smirking, sneering and starting to gather and fold papers before the meeting is over are all rude gestures.
- *Superiority of position*: Not responding or acknowledging others greetings, shouting orders, staring, standing too close, leaning or sitting on someone's desk, reclining in the chair with your hands folded behind your head, continuing to work as others speak to you, attending meetings with your mobile phone on, any unwarranted or unwanted touch, standing behind someone's seat and watching over his/her shoulder as he/she keeps working, a crushing handshake or keeping the hand held too long under your hand indicate your sense of superiority.

Body Shape

The physical shape of our body also communicates to others. We cannot do much about our physical structures, but by adopting the right kind of posture and dressing style, one can improve the impact of one's physical appearance. For example, standing up tall can help you to appear more authoritative, whereas a slumped posture or droopy shoulders create an appearance of passiveness or submissiveness.

Smell and Touch

Various odours and artificial fragrances on human beings can sometimes convey emotions and feelings better than words.

Smell: The non-verbal communication study of smell is known as Olfactics (OLFACTICS). Various odours and artificial fragrances on human beings can sometimes convey emotions and feelings better than words.

A smell can trigger the oldest of memories. We generally remember what we smell longer than what we see and hear.

Someone's smell can have a positive or negative effect on the oral message. This is because smell remains in the memory. People show a negative reaction to bad odours. It is really difficult to tell someone if he or she is smelling bad. The most common reaction is to avoid that person.

Especially in Western Europe and the US, personal hygiene is really important. In Japan, smell is very important. And Chinese people brame bad odour to eating a lot of meat.

Similarly, touching people in different ways can silently communicate friendship, love, disgust, approval or hatred. It is the context in which the touching is done which determines its implied sense. For example, a male doctor can touch any part of the female patient's body, but the patient does not object to the touching.

Touch is the mode of communicating intimacy. But which part of the body can be touched by whom and when depends upon the culture of the people of a country or a particular region. In western countries, as a gesture of appreciation, a superior in age and position can pat the back of an employee, both male and female; but in Asian countries like India, patting a lady on the back is not socially acceptable.

Silence

Silence can be a positive or negative influence in the communication process. It can provide a link between messages or break relationships. It can create uneasiness and tension or create a peaceful situation.

Advantages of understanding the non-verbal language are paramount. It strengthens your communicative competence as a professional. It means that you understand people and their meaning better. By gaining a fuller understanding of the message, you are better equipped to fulfill your purpose.

Non-verbal language has recently been shown to play an important role in two areas directly related to management: how managers motivate their employees, and how the executives communicate their leadership and decision-making styles.

However, one should not be completely dependent upon non-verbal language. One should also look into the matter and situation and analyse other aspects before reaching a conclusion.

SIGN LANGUAGE

The most basic element of communication is the sign. A sign is a symbol. A symbol is something that stands for something else. For example, a map is a symbol that represents an actual physical geographic territory, and the 21-gun salute is a symbol for respect. Symbols can be classified as visual symbols and audio symbols.

Visual Symbols

They are pictures, cartoons, paintings, maps, etc. which have a visual impact on the mind of the looker. Some symbols have a standard meaning throughout the world – like mathematical symbols, traffic signals, 'no smoking' signs, white flag denoting peace, etc.

Organisations make use of these symbols very often. There is the 'old man' symbol of 'The Times of India'. It represents the common man who reads this newspaper. We also have 'two hands coming from opposite directions to hold each other' of Nokia. It indicates connecting people all over the world. Not to forget, 'a strong man showing biceps' of MRF tyres' depicting strength and endurance of the tyres.

These symbols become synonymous with the organisation and communicate most important aspect of the the product of that organisation.

Colours play a crucial role in making the symbolic language rich. Red colour stands for hot, passion, blood, violence, anger. Green denotes fertility, environment, envy, money. White represents calmness, death, peace.

Advantages of visual communication are noteworthy. They communicate much in a short space and time, and get registered in the mind faster than words. There goes the famous saying – a picture saves a thousand words. Visual symbols are being frequently used in advertising and promotional campaigns.

However, a visual symbol has its own share of limitations too. It does not provide scope for interaction; its interpretation primarily depends upon the mindset and attitude of the person perceiving it. The person choosing symbols for communication must have a fair idea of the segment of people for whom it is meant and their possible reactions.

Audio Symbols

What do the following sounds mean to you? Morning alarm: time to wake up in the morning; siren: ambulance, police or fire extinguishing services; horn: giving way to other vehicles, etc.

These are the standard interpretations associated with these sounds which have been acquired by usage. These meaning rich symbols are some of the most powerful communication tools organisations have. Nowadays fire alarms are fitted in all the offices; sirens are generally used to convey lunch breaks in mills; bells are used by top-level managers to call their assistants or peons.

Sound symbols make communication much faster, economical and easy to organise. However, these signals have a limited use, and can be used to communicate simple and standard messages only.

PARALANGUAGE

You must have overheard two people arguing in the adjoining room. Even though you could not make out their words, their emotions and the fact that they were arguing was clear from the sound and tone of their voices. Similarly, when you hear two people talking in a language other than yours, though you are not abloe to understand the contents, you do get some idea about the talk and their feelings – if there was excitement, delight, frustration, anger, boredom or grief – from the tone of their voice and other non-verbal signs.

Paralanguage is the next closest thing to actual communication. It is the way we use our voice in uttering words. It is everything other than words – intonation, sarcasm, tone, pitch, etc.

Voice communicates in ways that has nothing to do with the words that the speaker utters. Sometimes words are pleasant, but the tone of the voice is harsh or sarcastic.

Given below are the various constituents of paralanguage :

- **Pitch variations:** Pitch of the voice means how high or low your vocal tones are. Use of pitch is in two contexts – firstly, using high or low pitch depending upon mind and emotions, and secondly, using variations in the pitch to make the talk more effective. The effect of different levels of pitch in the voice can be as follows :
  - **Monotone:** In a monotone the voice stays at the same pitch all the time, unrelated to the meaning of what is being said.
  - **Interesting:** Changes in the pitch level of certain words phrases can make the talk interesting for the listener as the

emotions can be felt through the speech. This change of pitch is called intonation.

- **Volume:** It refers to the loudness of the voice. A good speaker has to decide the volume of his/her speech
  - according to the place
  - according to the size of the audience
  - according to the meanings and emotions he/she wants to convey through the speech.

  Always remember that any departure from the average volume level will draw attention.
- **Speed and Pause:** Speed is another quality of voice. Speaking very fast will make the matter incomprehensible to the listener, and speaking at too low a speed will be boring. A normal pace should be maintained to get the message across clearly.
  Pauses are punctuation marks in speech. They are the speed breakers of language. They help to stress points and build interest.
- **Non-fluencies:** You must have come across people who use words and phrases like – OK, is it clear, that's great, isn't it, that's true, exactly, and so on. They sometimes make the talk better, and sometimes show lack of confidence in the speaker. It all depends on how frequently and at which places they are used.

CIRCUMSTANTIAL LANGUAGE

It is not the person alone who communicates. Everything about him/her and his/her surroundings communicates the way he walks, the way he dresses, the way he uses his time, the way he decorates his room, the way he allows people to enter the space around him etc.

Space language (Proxemics): It is actually 'personal space language'. Personal space is your 'bubble' – the space you place between yourself and others. This invisible boundary becomes clear only when someone bumps or tries to enter your bubble. The term 'proxemics' was coined by a researcher E.T. Hall in 1963.

1. **How the use of space communicates about our relationship with others:** The study of space for the purpose of communication involves four categories.
   - Intimate distance for embracing or whispering: physical contact to 18 inches.
   - Personal distance for conversation among close friends: 18 inches to 4 feet.
   - Social distance for conversations among acquaintances: 4 to 12 feet.

- Public distance used for public speaking: 12 feet to range of eyesight and hearing.

2. **How use of space communicates our status:** Interpersonal distance is a strong non-verbal indicator of power. There are three basic principles regarding the use of personal space in an organisation.
   - The higher your position or status, the more and better space you will have.
   - The better protected your territory will be.
   - It is easier to invade the territory of lower-status personnel.
3. **How use of space communicates the purpose of communication:** Consider 20 people sitting around a round table – seems to be a conference going on; a group of persons standing informally – seems to be a group of friends; arrangement having 100 chairs and a dais – seems to be a stage set for a lecture.

Space around a person can be informal as well as formal. From the organisation's viewpoint, it is fixed and semi-fixed space. In fixed space, the surrounding's physical features are fixed and cannot be changed on a routine basis, like the shape of the building, size and number of rooms. In semi-fixed space, there is scope for changing the physical settings – like the furniture, etc.

Time: Punctuality communicates a **lot**. It is considered a large part o good manners and civility. On the contrary, tardiness is viewed as a signal of hostility, procrastination and a relaxed attitude towards responsibility.

Surroundings: Different aspects of surroundings include room size, location, furnishings, machines, architecture, wall decorations, lighting, windows, the view, arrangement of objects in work area – desks, chairs, tables, bookcases, etc. Surroundings convey status.

Time: The way we use our time communicates a lot about us. Punctuality communicates a lot. The amount of time one spends on a task or problem is also an indicator of its importance. Moreover, the speed with which a task is finished communicates about its urgency.

APPEARANCE

Personal appearance plays a major role in judging a person simply because the first impression of a person is based on appearance. People can change their appearance by changing their clothing styles, hairstyles, accessories and artifacts. This channel of non-verbal communication is transmitted through the following.

1. **Physical characteristics:** These include facial shape, body shape, height, skin colour, body odour, hair, deformities, etc.
2. **Attire:** It refers to clothing and accessories. They are powerful signifiers and convey a great deal about someone's job, personality, values and lifestyle. Generally, people are treated on the basis of the social status their dress indicates.

To establish credibility, wear styles that fit the environment and are comfortable. Your dress should flatter your body type.

Adornments and accessories are another form of appearance which also takes into accounts personal grooming.

It is important to

- ❑ pay attention to good grooming, which involves a neat hairstyle, body hygiene, polished shoes, and clean nails.
- ❑ invest in professional looking clothing and accessories.
- ❑ avoid flashy garments, over the top jewellery, loud make up and overpowering perfumes.

Communication is more than verbal. In fact verbal exchanges account for only a fraction of the messages people send and receive. Research has shown that between 70 and 90 per cent of the entire communication is non-verbal.

POINTS TO REMEMBER

- Communication is classified into verbal and non-verbal communication.
- When words are used in communication, be it spoken (oral) or written, it is termed as verbal communication.
- Non-verbal communication includes facial expressions, eye contact, tone of voice, body posture and motions, and positioning within groups. It may also include the way one wears clothes or remains silent.
- Different types of non-verbal communication are: body language, sign language, paralanguage, circumstantial language.
- Body language is the way the body communicates by its physical movements.
- Sign language makes use of symbols – visual and audio.
- Paralanguage is the way we use our voice in uttering words.
- Circumstantial language makes use of the space, surroundings and time, and plays an important role in effective non-verbal communication.
- Personal appearance is a major factor used to judge a person simply because the first impression of a person is based on appearance.

Chapter

3

Barriers to Effective Communication

Learning Objectives

- To understand the possible barriers that can distort communication
- To understand the barriers on the part of the sender and ways to overcome them
- To understand the barriers on the part of the receiver and ways to overcome them
- To understand the barriers on the part of the organisation and ways to overcome them

No one would talk much in society if they knew how often they misunderstood others.

—Johann Wolfgang Von Goethe

Communication is successful only when the receiver understands the message intended by the sender. Interference in the communication process that distorts or obscures the sender's meaning is called 'noise'. Such noise can be caused by a variety of communication barriers. A manager must understand the source of these barriers to communication so that it can be properly dealt with.

BARRIERS ON PART OF SENDER

1. **Faulty planning:** The pre-requisite of effective communication is planning. The message should be properly planned and then delivered. The contents of the message should be clear in the mind of the sender and the appropriate medium or channel should be chalked out.
2. **Vague presumptions:** Leaving gaps in the message, with the assumption that the receiver will understand what has actually been conveyed, leads to confusion and chaos, further leading to non-effective communication. Unclarified and unshared assumptions can become a major barrier.
3. **Semantics:** Semantics is the science that deals with the meaning of words. People assign different meanings to words. Which means that it is possible for one word to have different meanings to two pesons. If the sender and the receiver choose words with same meanings assigned, then communication is perfect. Since the same words may have different meanings to different people, the sender should strive to use words that conform with the receiver's experiences and attitudes.
4. **Poorly expressed contents:** Sometimes, the sender is clear in his mind about the message, but due to lack of command over the use of appropriate and exact words, the meaning gets lost.
5. **Emotional factors:** Feelings like prejudice, threat, foul mood, aggression, hatred distort communication.
6. **Emphasising the wrong part of the message:** Not stressing the key point of the message leads to confusion. Sometimes you must have come across advertisements where the focus is on everything but the product, thereby leading to confusion as to what the product being advertised was.
7. **Inconsistent verbal and non-verbal communication:** When our words and body language are giving conflicting signals, the message gets distorted. For example, when a subordinate is saying 'everything is fine', but not maintaining eye contact,

he/she is definitely either trying to hide something or is not sure about the words.

8. **Filtering:** It is the deliberate manipulation of information to make it appear more favourable to the receiver. For example, when an individual tells his boss what he wants to hear, it is filtering information.

OVERCOMING BARRIERS ON PART OF SENDER

1. **Planning and clarifying the ideas:** The ideas should be planned ahead and be clear in the mind. The right channel or medium to impart the message should also be chalked out for communication to the effective.
2. **Overcoming different perceptions:** Whenever possible, the sender should try to learn about the background of the receiver and his/her knowledge of the subject. This will help in using familiar terms. Also, empathising with the receiver will help in communicating better.
3. **Overcoming semantic problems:** It is helpful if the receiver asks the meaning of unconventional and technical terms, and confirms or restates the main points of the message.
4. **Overcoming the inconsistencies between verbal and non-verbal language:** Gestures, facial expressions, postures, clothes and other powerful non-verbal language should agree with the verbal language.
5. **Overcoming the emotional factor:** Primarily, the sender should be aware of his emotional moods and how they might influence others before communicating an important message. This helps in the transmission of the message without any psychological and emotional obstacles.
6. **Minimising distractions:** Eliminate physical distractions such as the messy appearance of a written message or poor acoustics in an oral presentation. Overcome emotional barriers by using neutral words which do not arouse strong feelings.

BARRIERS ON PART OF RECEIVER

1. **Distractions:** This could be in the form of the speaker itself, some physical noise like a roaring bike crossing by, music playing in the background, health problems, or some other irritating condition. Emotional distractions have a greater potential for creating misunderstandings. If the receiver is emotional, he may

ignore or distort the message depending upon the emotions involved.

2. **Poor listening:** Listening requires attention and patience. It requires the listener to avoid making premature evaluations of what the speaker has to say. When the receiver is inattentive, or not listening due to boredom, uninteresting subject, or prejudice against the speaker, the message gets lost.
3. **Psychological factors:** Factors like closed minds, rigid beliefs and non-flexible approach towards receiving new information or ideas distorts the message in the communication process.
4. **Prejudice or distrust against the speaker:** When the receiver of the message views the sender with distrust and bias, he doubts the credibility of the message, irrespective of its contents. Thus, the message is never well taken.

OVERCOMING BARRIERS ON PART OF RECEIVER

1. **Focus on the message, not the speaker:** A preconceived opinion of the speaker hinders the receiver to take the message properly. Besides personal bias, some receivers also judge the speaker by his manners and attitudes, outer physical appearance, facial expressions and body language. All this could affect the acceptance of the message.
2. **Overcoming poor listening:** Developing a habit of active listening and concentrating on the message can lead to greater understanding of the message conveyed by the sender. It would involve patience to listen till the matter is concluded without attempts to disrupt, stopping the mind from wandering away and empathising with the speaker.
3. **Open mind:** Being approachable and having a broad mindset leads to effective communication. One should lay aside preconceived opinions and be open to new ideas and information.

BARRIERS ON PART OF ORGANISATION

1. **Restrictive environment:** Every link in the communication chain is open to error. So, by the time a message travels all the way through a chain, it gets distorted and bears little resemblance to the original idea. If a company's formal communication network limits the flow of information in any direction (upward, downward or horizontal), communication becomes fragmented. Authoritarian management style also prevents free flow of

communication because of a lack of management interest and a lack of effective means for sharing their ideas.

2. **Insufficient time period:** Managers are generally hard pressed for time. This leads to disruption in communication channels because sufficient time is not given to understand and digest the message.

3. **Organisational structure:** It has an important influence on the ability of the members of the organisation to communicate effectively. Modern businesses are complex involving several layers. They, in turn, create problems because communication may break down at any level due to faulty transmission.

4. **Cultural barriers:** An organisation comprises of innumerable people belonging to different cultures which shapes behaviour and understanding of a person. Culture can be defined as a set of values, beliefs, norms, customs, rules and codes with which a person can identify himself. Sometimes, cultural variations may act as a barrier due to perceptual or language differences.

5. **Perceptual and language differences:** Even when two people have experienced the same event, their mental images of that event will not be identical. Because perceptions are unique, the ideas expressed also differ from people to people. As a sender, you choose details that seem important to you, a process known as selective perception. As a receiver, you try to fit in new details into your existing pattern. If a detail does not fit, you are inclined to distort the information.

   Language comprises of words, which have been assigned different meanings by different people. Words are taken either for their denotative value (dictionary meaning) or connotative value (assigned meanings). Some words have positive connotations, others have negative — it all depends on an individual's unique experiences and attitudes.

6. **Deceptive tactics:** Deceptive communicators may exaggerate benefits, quote inaccurate statistics, or hide negative information behind an optimistic attitude. They may leave out crucial information and portray graphic data unfairly. Moreover, they allow personal preferences to influence their own perception and the perception of others. Using deceptive tactics to manipulate receivers blocks the communication and leads to failure.

7. **Information overload:** Today's individual is burdened by message overload. The content ranges from urgent messages and

information to trivial ones to chitchat and jokes. The huge number of messages is distracting making it difficult to differentiate between useful and useless information. Many companies nowadays are dealing with this information overload by encouraging employees to send fewer messages and discouraging the use of the word 'urgent'.

OVERCOMING BARRIERS ON PART OF ORGANISATION

1. **Adopt an audience centered approach:** Using this approach means keeping your audience in mind at all times when communicating, thereby caring about them, and making the message meaningful to them. Try to know about the background and knowledge of the audience so that you can communicate with them in familiar terms.
2. **Choosing the right medium or channel:** A message can be conveyed using different channels. Choosing the right kind of medium depending upon the kind and purpose of the message, and the level of people to whom the message is intended, will help overcome the barriers.
3. **Open communication atmosphere:** The organisation must make sure that communication flows freely up, down and across. It should encourage frankness and honesty, and the employees must feel free to confess their mistakes, disagree with the boss, and express their opinions.
4. **Simplify the number of organisational levels:** The number of levels in the organisation structure should be reduced. The fewer the links in the communication chain, the less the communication will break down leading to faulty transmission and misunderstandings. This will enable the managers to share information with colleagues and employees and participate in decision-making, goal setting and problem solving.
5. **Feedback:** Feedback is the reaction; without it the sender of the message cannot know whether the recipient has received the message properly and grasped its meaning accurately. Encourage feedback by asking specific questions, encourage the audience to express reactions, and be receptive to the audience's response.
6. **Create lean and efficient messages:** Too much information is as bad as too little – it reduces the audience's ability to concentrate on the most important data. Differentiation must be made between useful and useless information. Organisations save time and money by sending only necessary messages.

POINTS TO REMEMBER

- Communication is successful only when the receiver understands the message intended by the sender. Interference in the communication process is caused by a variety of communication barriers.
- A barrier can occur at any point of time in the course of communication process – on the part of the sender, receiver or organisation.
- These barriers can be overcome once the source of the barrier is identified. Efforts have to be made by all constituents – sender, receiver and organisation.
- Awareness about the communication barriers and ways of overcoming them certainly helps to improve communication.

Chapter

4

Listing Skills

Learning Objectives

- To understand how important listening is in oral communication
- To undetstand the difference between hearing and listening
- To undetstand the concept of the listening process
- To get familiar with barriers to effective listening
- To know the guidelines for effective listening
- To know the various types of listening
- To become an effective listener

The most basic and powerful way to connect to another person is to listen. Just listen.

Perhaps the most important thing we ever give each other is our attention... a loving silence often has far more power to heal and to connect than the most well-intentioned words.

—Rachel Naomi Remen

INTRODUCTION

Nature blessed us with two ears but only one tongue, which is a gentle hint that we should listen more than we talk. To listen actively to another human being may be the greatest gift you can give a person. For a long time, people assumed that listening was a natural trait, but practically speaking, not all people are good listeners. Listening is a skill that must be developed.

Listening can be defined as 'the ability to understand and respond effectively to oral communication.' Your ability to listen effectively is directly related to your success in interpersonal relationships. Unfortunately, most people are not good listeners. Most of us face so many distractions while listening that we often give speakers less than our full attention. Furthermore, when questioned about what we have just heard, we get all the facts mixed up. This happens because one tends to listen to words and not to the message.

DIFFERENCE BETWEEN HEARING AND LISTENING

Many people take it for granted that they are good listeners. One must make a distinction between listening and hearing. Most people often confuse listening with picking up sound vibrations which is only hearing; listening is concerned with making sense or meaning out of what we hear.

Hearing is a physical and listening a mental process. Hearing is passive, while listening is active. Hearing involves just receiving sound signals, but listening requires the use of ears, brain, eyes to understand non-verbal cues, with additional insights like perception, attitudes and participation, etc.

THE LISTENING PROCESS

Listening often involves five steps: receiving, interpreting, remembering, evaluating, and responding.

1. **Receiving:** Physically hearing the message and taking note of it is 'receiving'. Physical reception can be blocked by noise, impaired hearing, or inattention.
2. **Interpreting:** Assigning meaning to sounds according to one's own values, beliefs, ideas, expectations, roles, needs and personal history in 'interpreting'. The point to note here is that the interpreted meaning may differ from that of the speaker's intended meaning.
3. **Remembering:** Storing a message for future reference is 'remembering'. It is easier to retain what one hears by taking notes or making a mental outline.

4. **Evaluating:** Applying critical thinking skills to weigh the speaker's remarks is 'evaluating'.
5. **Responding:** Reacting once the speaker's message is evaluated is the 'response'.

BARRIERS TO EFFECTIVE LISTENING

1. **Prejudice against the speaker:** When we do not hold the speaker in a good light, the listening process is lost.
2. **Rehearsing:** Your whole attention is on designing and preparing your next comment and not on listening. You are thinking about what to say next.
3. **Identifying:** Self-centredness is the root cause of identifying. It takes people to take control of conversations, rather than listening to what is being said. They shift the attention from the speakers to themselves.
4. **Advising:** People start advising without listening to the content. They become the great problem solver.
5. **Rebuttal instinct:** In this case the main focus is on finding things to disagree with. People listen to find flaws.
6. **Distraction:** The distractions can be external, internal, physical or mental. It can be the personal mood of the speaker, noisy fans, glaring lights, background music, overheated or cold rooms, a conversation going on nearby, thinking about a domestic problem, pressed for time, atmosphere, etc.
7. **Lack of motivation:** Listening requires time, physical, and mental energy. Unless people are motivated, they do not spend their time, energy and anything. Unfamiliar speaker, unrelated subject, ineffective speech, lack of faith and confidence can prove to be non- motivating.
8. **Wandering mind:** Most of us speak at 60 to 180 words per minute, and people have the capacity to think at 500 to 800 words per minute. The difference leaves us with ample spare time and the mind wanders or takes mental excursions.
9. **Delivery:** Effective listening is not possible if the delivery is monotonous. It can put listeners to sleep or cause them to loose interest.
10. **Taking notes:** People commonly take notes while listening, which, in turn, reduces their listening capacity. A good listener's approach is to listen carefully and write down only the key points or leading ideas.

11. **False listening:** Pseudo listeners make the speaker believe that they are listening. They appear to be listening but are not actually involved in the process of listening, interpreting and understanding the message.
12. **Monologues:** There are people who are egocentric or self-centred and prefer talking about themselves rather than sharing in a conversation. Monologue is a long speech by one person.
13. **Selective listening:** In selective listening, also known as out-listening, you let your mind wander to other things or you tune out until you hear a word or phrase that gets your attention. Some listeners concentrate and pick out only those aspects which interest them and reject other things.
14. **Listening defensively:** People who are very sensitive take everything as a personal attack. It is known as listening defensively and acts as a barrier to effective listening.
15. **Noise:** Noise is anything that hangs like a cloud over the entire communication environment. It is anything and everything that distracts a listener from understanding a message.
16. **Closed mind:** It refers to the thinking tendency of people who have rigid beliefs about everything and are not open to new ideas and information. This proves as a barrier to effective listening.

GUIDELINES FOR EFFECTIVE LISTENING

1. **Eye contact:** When the individual does not look at the speaker, it means he or she is not interested in listening. A listener must maintain an eye contact as it encourages the speaker.
2. **Bodily exhibitions:** A listener must show that he is interested in listening by giving non-verbal signs like nodding of the head, appropriate facial expressions and a smile now and then.
3. **Resist distractions:** Tune out external and internal distractions by facing and maintaining contact with the speaker. You can close doors, turn off the radio or television, or move closer to the speaker. Avoid distracting gestures like looking at your watch now and then, shuffling papers, playing with pen, pencil, etc.
4. **Ask questions:** An effective listener always asks questions, clarifies doubts, seeks explanations and ensures clear understanding.

5. **Paraphrasing:** Restating in one's own words what the speaker has said is called paraphrasing. Firstly, it acts as a control over listening, and secondly, it ensures accuracy.
6. **Do not interrupt and overtake:** Some people, instead of listening to the speaker till he completes his version, speak their own ideas or points. An effective listener will never overtake the speaker, because he knows that one cannot talk and listen at the same time.
7. **Keep an open mind:** A good listener does not feel threatened or insulted, nor does he resist messages that contradict his beliefs, values, opinions or ideas.
8. **Avoid arguments:** Hold your rebuttal until you have heard the entire message. Don't allow your personal biases and attitudes to influence your listening to the message.
9. **Find an area of interest:** Good listeners are interested and attentive. They find ways to make the message relevant to them.
10. **Empathise with the speaker:** Empathy means placing yourself in the shoes of the speaker and trying to understand his viewpoint. By showing empathy, the listener creates a climate that encourages others to communicate openly and honestly.
11. **Hold your temper:** Be patient. Don't interrupt. Don't become over-stimulated and excited too soon by what the speaker is saying. Be sure that you have understood what the speaker is saying and hold your judgment till the message is completed.

TYPES OF LISTENING

Different situations call for different listening skills. To be a good listener, vary the way you listen to suit the situation. The following types of listening differ not only in purpose but also in the amount of feedback or interaction that occurs :

1. **Evaluative listening:** Also known as critical listening, it means that the listener while listening to the message spares time and thinks while judging and evaluating what is being said, and sometimes forms arguments and rebuttals to it. This type of listening generally involves interaction.
2. **Projective listening:** Also known as content listening, it is more commonly used in meetings and other types of group communication. It is a process of observing and understanding what is said and assimilating the viewpoint of the speaker. Listeners have to fully grasp the message and the emotional

contents of the ideas. In this type of listening judgment passing is not an important aspect.

3. **Active listening:** Also known as empathic listening, the goal is to understand the speaker's feelings, needs and wants so that you can appreciate his or her point of view, regardless of whether you share that perspective. Active listening consists of listening to a person without passing judgment on what is being said, and to mirror back what has been said to indicate that you understood what feelings the speaker was putting across. The idea is to avoid the temptation to give advice and just let the other person talk.

WHAT DO GOOD LISTENERS DO?

Good listeners pay attention, focus on the speaker in a generous way rather than on themselves, avoid making assumptions, and listen for feelings as well as facts.

- **Pay attention:** Good listening requires energy. Distractions have to be resisted and noise tuned out. Some listening errors happen because the listner was not paying enough attention to a key point. To avoid listening errors caused by inattention take note of the following :
  - Before the meeting, anticipate the answers you need to get. Make a list of your questions. During the conversation, listen for answers to your questions.
  - At the end, check your understanding with some other person; especially check who does what next.
- **Focus on the speaker in a generous way:** Some people listen looking for flaws. They focus on other things rather than on the message. Good listeners are generous. Rather than pointing out the first error they hear and tuning out the speaker while they wait impatiently for their own turn to speak, good listeners weigh all the evidence before they come to a judgment. They realise that they can learn something even from people they do not like.
  - Focus on the message rather than the speaker.
  - Spend your time evaluating what the speaker says, not planning your rebuttal.
  - Learn something from every speaker.
- **Avoid making assumptions:** Many listening errors arise from faulty assumptions. Asking questions can be helpful. Remember the following to avoid faulty assumptions.

- Do not ignore instructions you think are unnecessary.
- Consider the speaker's background and experiences to understand that why this point is important to him and what might he or she mean by it.
- Paraphrase what the speaker has said, giving him or her a chance to correct your understanding.

- **Listen for feelings and facts:** Empathise with the speaker to understand his or her situation and feelings.
  - Pay attention to non-verbal signs like tone of voice, facial expressions and body language.
  - Don't assume that silence means consent. Invite the other person to speak.

POINTS TO REMEMBER

- Listening can be defined as 'the ability to understand and respond effectively to oral communication.'
- Hearing is through the ears and listening is through the mind.
- Listening often involves five steps: receiving, interpreting, remembering, evaluating, and responding.
- For improving the listening skill, overcoming barriers that disrupt the listening process is necessary.
- The types of listening – evaluative, projective and active – differ not only in purpose but also in the amount of feedback or interaction that occurs.
- Good listeners pay attention, focus on the speaker in a generous way rather than on themselves, avoid making assumptions, and listen for feelings as well as facts.

Chapter

5

Group Communication/Meetings

Learning Objectives

- To understand the concept of a group and its distinct personality
- To understand the difference between formal and informal groups
- To understand the various types of groups
- To understand the role of communication in groups
- To learn how group discussions can be made effective
- To understand the process of group decision-making and various group techniques used
- To understand the concept of meetings
- To learn how to conduct meetings
- To learn the relevance and preparation of agenda, notice and minutes in a meeting
- To learn how to draft the resolutions passed in a meeting
- To understand procedures before, during and after the meeting
- To understand the roles of group members/participants

If anything goes bad, I did it. If anything goes semigood, we did it. If anything goes really good, then you did it. That's all it takes to get people to win football games for you.

—Paul William "Bear" Bryant

WHAT IS A GROUP?

A group is formally defined as a small collection of people who interact with each other, usually face to face, over time in order to reach goals.

A group is more than simply a collection of people. But what exactly is it that makes a group a group? Some of the key characteristics of a group are as given below :

- **Interaction:** Without interaction, a collection of people is not a group. This requirement of interaction highlights the difference between true groups and collections of individuals who merely engage in a similar activity without communicating with each other. For example, students who passively listen to a lecture do not technically constitute a group, until they begin to exchange messages with each other and their instructor.
- **Interdependence:** In groups, members do not just interact, they are interdependent. The behaviour of one person affects all the others – be it positive or negative. When one member behaves poorly or successfully, his or her actions shape the way the entire group functions.
- **Time:** A collection of people who interact for a short while does not qualify as a group. The element of time clearly excludes temporary gatherings.
- **Size:** Most experts in the field set the lower limit of group size at three members. It is often stressed that the optimal size for a group is the smallest number of people capable of performing the task at hand effectively. The optimal number will change according to the task.
- **Goals:** People usually hope to achieve one or more goals when they join a group. The groups have a common goal through which all their members identify themselves in a common context.
- **Group culture:** Culture refers to the patterns of values, beliefs, norms and behaviour shared by the members of a group. Each small group is unique. No two groups develop the same pattern of norms and behaviour.
- **Collective power:** Group denotes collective power. It gives a feeling to the member that he or she is not alone in their pursuits. Furthermore, a strong group or a more cohesive group becomes a power unit.

Why Groups?

One man cannot fight with the whole world. Groups are inevitable in any enterprise; there need cannot be ignored or denied

- **Formal Groups** are formed by organisations to accomplish set goals: they are useful in the decision making process. Group solutions to problems tend to be better than the solutions offered by separate individuals. In addition, there are problems for which acceptance by the group is particularly important for effective implementation.
- **Informal Groups** emerge because of the social nature of human beings: they are not deliberately formed but emerge when people with some common interests interact. An informal group helps its members by giving them a forum to express themselves emotionally, and a feeling of recognition and support.

Types of Groups

1. **Learning groups:** Although academic settings certainly qualify as learning groups, they are not the only ones. Whatever the setting or subject, the purpose of learning groups is to increase the knowledge or skill of each member.
2. **Problem-solving groups:** These groups work to resolve the mutual concerns of members. Sometimes the problem involves the group itself, and at other times, the problem is external to the group.
3. **Social groups:** Man is a social animal. These groups satisfy the social needs of their participants.

How are Groups Formed?

Most groups go through four formative stages :

- **Forming:** Here the group tries to get started. It is the orientation phase for group members.
- **Storming:** Members begin to stake out their positions and begin to have conflicts and arguments.
- **Norming:** Progress begins here. Members work to solve conflicts.
- **Performing:** Here the group begins to achieve its goals.

GROUP COMMUNICATION

Group communication is defined as the interaction of a group of people to achieve an interdependent goal. Members of a group interact in such a way that each can influence and be influenced by others. This interaction occurs through communication, which is usually face to face, but other channels of communication such as computer network can also qualify. Communication facilitates interaction among group members and is an essential process within a group.

- **Communication creates and maintains groups:** Communication creates a group in the very first place, shapes each group in a unique way, and then maintains it. The communication among members is what creates group rules and operating procedures.
- **Facilitates sharing information:** Information – whether it is data about sales performance, or instructions on how to perform a task – is the core of group communication.
- **Facilitates interpersonal relationships:** Communication facilitates the emotional expression of feelings and fulfillment of social needs. It also helps in building trust and acceptance.
- **Acts to regulate, motivate and control employees in several ways:** Downward communication guides an employee as to what is expected of him and how the job should be done. Upward communication facilitates in conveying the suggestions, queries, grievances, etc. of the employees to the management. Many motivational and control techniques can be used by communicating only.
- **Facilitates decision-making:** Communication provides the information that individuals and groups need to make decisions by transmitting the data to identify and evaluate alternative choices.

Effective Group Communication

The following six steps need to be followed to make group communication effective :

1. **Planning:** The planning for a discussion – identifying what the problem to be discussed is, who should be called for discussion, what is supposed to be achieved by the discussion, who is going to lead it – makes the communication more result-oriented and relevant.
2. **Clarity of purpose:** It is very important to define the purpose. If the members of the group are clear about the what and why of the issue, then wastage of time can be avoided.
3. **Leadership:** In a group communication, people themselves take different roles depending upon their capabilities, skills and mindsets. But throughout all this, a leader is required to keep the

discussion on track. The leader may be a formally designated one, or may emerge within the group setting due to his/her personal qualities.

4. **Participation:** The purpose of forming groups is to make use of knowledge and expertise of different persons. If the group members do not participate, then the very purpose of forming groups will be defeated.
5. **Use familiar words:** Use conventional sentences so that people understand you better. Avoid the use of jargons and use familiar language keeping in mind the background and attitudes of the group members.
6. **Speak concisely:** Don't give long speeches. Don't monopolise the conversation and let others share their bit too.

GROUP DECISION MAKING

One of the most obvious applications of groups is to solve problems, because groups have the potential to work better than individuals. The information is communicated fast and then used in decision making. Moreover, group decisions require transmitting of message between members, and the effectiveness of this communication process will significantly impact the quality of group decisions. The group decision making process involves the following steps :

1. Identifying the problem
2. Analysing the problem
3. Developing creative solutions through brainstorming
4. Evaluating the solutions
5. Implementing the plan
6. Following up on the best solution

There are several approaches a group can use to make decisions. They are as follows :

- **Consensus:** Consensus occurs when all members of the group support a decision. It is especially important in decisions on critical or complex matters. The advantages are full participation, which increases the quality of the decision, as well as the commitment of the members to support it. The disadvantages being that it takes a great deal of time, making it unsuitable for emergencies.
- **Majority control:** This method has its advantages in matters where support of all members is not necessary, but in more

important matters it is risky. Moreover, it also produces unhappy members who eventually participate less.

- **Expert opinion:** Sometimes one group member is defined as an expert and is given the power to take decisions. There is often disagreement on the question as to who is an expert. Sometimes, a member may think that he or she is the best qualified to take a decision, but others might disagree.
- **Minority control:** Sometimes few members of a group decide matters. This approach works well with non-critical questions that would waste the whole group's time. In the form of a committee, a minority of members can also study an issue in greater detail than the entire group.
- **Authority rule:** It is the approach often used by autocratic leaders. There are times when this approach has its advantages too, like sometimes when there is no time for a group to decide what to do. It is also acceptable in routine matters where approval of the entire group is not needed. But the disadvantages are hard to ignore. This approach 'when overused' can create problems. The failure to consult with members can lead to decrease in efficiency even when the leader's decision is a reasonable one.

Group Decision-Making Techniques

Some commonly used techniques of group problem solving are as follows :

1. **Brainstorming:** Brainstorming is an idea generation process. Under this technique, group members are encouraged to generate ideas to solve the given problems. These ideas may range from wild to sophisticated ones. The objective is not to restrict the thinking process by putting limitations. It is useful for generating many ideas in a short time.
2. **Nominal group technique:** It is a technique where goals are set and the problems are identified before the group. The members independently work upon the problem and note down their ideas without any discussion thereon. Thereafter these ideas are collected and discussed by the group for clarity and evaluation.
3. **Delphi technique:** This technique has emerged out of modern day requirements where concerned persons find it difficult to gather physically to constitute a decision making group. The problem is identified and people give their views independently thereon which are reconciled at a central place, and such

reconciled views are again reflected upon the members individually. This process is repeated till an optimal decision is reached.

This technique is useful when the group participants are at diverse physical locations and it is a very time consuming and expensive affair to call them physically at a central location.

4. **Meetings:** The very fact that a group has to take decisions requires meeting of group members. The style of meetings can vary enormously – from informal to formal, from highly controlled to free, from personal to impersonal. Meeting provides a group decision-making forum. A meeting would be considered as being effective when its purpose is accomplished, that is, where the subject of the meeting is discussed in the meeting to give some constructive results.

   Meetings have two core purposes – to present information and help solve problems. Two kinds of meetings help achieve these objectives :

   - **Informational meetings:** They seek only to clarify, to make something clear and to give information. For example, announcement of the new mission statement of the company, report on the company's strategic plans for the next financial year, etc. In these types of meetings, no problems are solved and no recommendations for change occur. Participants just came to the meeting with one purpose – to be informed.
   - **Problem solving meetings:** In these types of meetings, the major problem is presented before the group of participants, who suggest solutions and suggestions. Then the discussion and evaluation is carried on and the participants arrive at a decision for further action.

Out of the four group decision-making techniques mentioned here, we shall take up meetings in detail.

MEETING PROCEDURES

By meeting procedures, it is implied the procedures adopted to facilitate and record the proceedings of a meeting. The documentation part is as follows :

Agenda

Agenda is a list of topics covered in the meeting. A well-prepared agenda will assist the chairperson in directing the business of meeting and ensuring that decisions are reached in an efficient manner. A well organised and constructed agenda forms the basis for a good meeting, and this, in turn, makes it easier to write the minutes.

The characteristics of an agenda are :

- It is usually a part of the notice of the meeting.
- It is fixed beforehand and lists all items or matters that will be taken up for discussion. It can also be accompanied by necessary papers, notes, data, etc.
- It usually contains the name of the organisation, venue, date and time as well as the nature of meeting.

Agendum

Every individual item on the agenda is called as agendum. Each agendum should :

- have a clear and concise heading.
- state the issue and its source.
- provide essential background information.

Given below is an example of an agendum.

Ashish is the managing director of XYZ Pvt. Ltd. They are planning to open a new branch in Hyderabad. Ashish has to call a meeting to finalise office equipment, decoration and promotion plans.

AGENDA

Date: 15th October, 2008

To: Anu Sharma, Rahul Sharma, Raman Singh, Alka

From: Ashish Chauhan

Subject: Planning meeting for new Hyderabad office

Time/Place: Saturday, 1st November, 2008 from 9:30 A.M. to 11:30 A.M. in the Board room.

Background: We are still on a target of 1st January, 2009 as opening date for the Hyderabad office. Completing the tasks below will keep us on the right track.

We will discuss the following items/issues:

1. *Office equipment*: Please come with a list of business equipment you think will be needed for the office. At the meeting, we will standardise the purchases as much as possible.
2. *Office decoration*: We have hired a professional designer from Wizcraft design group. She will present a preliminary design for our approval.

3. *Promotions/Marketing strategies*: Rahul Sharma wants to prepare a series of press releases for distribution to Wizcraft media a month or so before the office opens. Please come with suggestions of items needed to be included in this list.

Notice of a Meeting

After deciding the contents (agenda) of the meeting, the next step is to give a notice of the meeting to all the participants. This notice informs the members about the date, venue, time and issues to be discussed in the meeting. It should be ensured that the notice is well-circulated before the date of the meeting, so that the members can plan their participation in the meeting.

Notice intimating the information may be given in two ways. The given below are two examples to explain both the ways :

1. A notice mentioning place, date and time of the meeting is given to the members, and a copy of the agenda is attached with the notice.

XYZ Pvt. Ltd.

Address: Barakhamba Road,

Connaught Circus, New Delhi

NOTICE

Notice is hereby given that the 5th meeting of the Board of Directors will be held at the registered office of the company (the above mentioned address), at 9:30 A.M., on Monday, 10th November, 2008.

The agenda is attached.

Ramesh Goel

Secretary

To the members of

the board of directors

Dated: 01-11-2008

Place: New Delhi

2. The agenda itself is prepared in such a way that it provides all the information required to be given in the notice.

XYZ Pvt. Ltd.
Address: Barakhamba Road,
Connaught Circus, New Delhi

NOTICE

Notice is hereby given that the 5th meeting of the Board of Directors will be held at the registered office of the company (the above mentioned address), at 9:30 A.M., on Monday, 10th November, 2008, to transact the following business:

1. To adopt the annual accounts together with the auditors report and directors report thereon.
2. To appoint Amita Sharma as the new Sales Manager.
3. To appoint the L.N. Bansal & Co., Chartered Accountants as auditors upto the conclusion of the next annual general meeting.

On behalf of the Board
For XYZ Pvt. Ltd.

Ramesh Goel
Secretary

To the members of
the board of directors

Dated: 01-11-2008
Place: New Delhi

Minutes of a Meeting

During the course of a meeting, the items or topics listed in the agenda are discussed serially one by one. All the participants express their views/opinions and discuss amongst themselves the advantages and disadvantages of each issue of agenda. Finally, they arrive at some conclusions or decisions, which are always kept on official record. This documentation is called as minutes of a meeting. In other words, minutes are the formal records of proceedings of a meeting.

The purpose of writing minutes is

- to serve as the formal record of the discussion
- to serve as a background or reference for future discussions.

The minutes of a meeting contain

- Date and number of meeting
- A list of people who attended the meeting
- A list of members who did not attend the meeting
- The essential, relevant background to the topic under discussion
- A summary of the discussion
- A clear record of the decision/resolution reached, and the names of individuals/ bodies that were responsible for it.

The following points should be kept in mind while writing the minutes :

- Be brief and concise.
- Be clear. Clarity is essential. Those who were not present should be able to understand what happened at the meeting from reading the minutes. Decisions or resolutions should be conveyed clearly and the actual language should be produced.
- The minutes should be self-contained and sufficient in themselves so that no additional information is required if they are referred to by someone.
- The minutes should be recorded immediately after the meeting.

Resolutions Passed in a Meeting

When decisions are taken in formal meetings, they are known as resolutions, meaning thereby that the members of the meeting have resolved the matter by deciding on the given course of action. When these decisions are mentioned in the minutes, they are presented in the form of resolutions.

- Decisions which are within the power of the committee are introduced by the words – "**It was resolved that....**"
- Sometimes the members of the meeting are not empowered to take a decision on the given topic. They can only recommend their opinion to the higher authority who can take the decision. They are recorded as "**It was resolved to recommend....**"

Look at the example of the minutes of a meeting with resolutions as given below :

Minutes of the 15th meeting of ABC Pvt. Ltd. held on Sunday, 10th August, 2008 at the Regd. Office of the company at 240, Tughlaqabad, New Delhi, at 10:00 A.M.

Present:

Mr Anil Jain

Mr Sachin Sharma

Ms Anu Sharma

Mr Rohit Gandhi

The following members did not attend the meeting:

Ms Shikha Gupta

Mr Amit Sana

Mr Sumit Khanna

The following matters/business were taken up at the Meeting and the resolutions passed.

It was resolved that Mr Amrish Arora be and hereby appointed as the General Manager of the company with effect from 11.09.2008, at a consolidated salary of Rs. 50,000 p.m. and other benefits as per rules of the company.

It was resolved that the permanent staff members of the company, who have served the company for complete 5 years, be sanctioned and granted up to a maximum of Rs 5 lakh individually as housing loan for purchase of land or constructing building at a nominal interest of 4% p.a. with a repayment not exceeding ten years.

Employment contract – Mr Sharma suggested some minor changes in the employment contract of the company, which was agreed by the committee. Since the changes are to be approved by the Managing Director, **it was resolved to recommend** omitting Clause 6 of the employment contract to the managing contract.

No other matter was discussed in the meeting. The meeting concluded with a vote of thanks to the chairperson.

Chairperson

Place:

Dated:

Planning Steps Before the Meeting

As a group leader, you should be prepared for the upcoming meeting in the following ways :

- ❑ Review the problem and determine the precise purpose
- ❑ Decide who should participate
- ❑ Arrange for meeting date, time and place
- ❑ Create an agenda
- ❑ Distribute the announcement for the meeting
- ❑ Check on physical arrangements.

Procedures During the Meeting

- ❑ Begin with a neutral, bias free opening statement which can start the session on a positive note.
- ❑ Stimulate discussion. Involving all members in a discussion is central to a leader's responsibilities.
- ❑ Understand the roles of the participants.
- ❑ State the major conclusions and plan of action.

Follow up After the Meeting

Secretaries take minutes, leaders or chairpersons check for accuracy.

Follow up after the meeting: As follow up, e-mail an atachment of the meeting notes to each of the participants. This way, all the meeting participants have access to the meeting notes if there is an idea or discussion they would like to revisit.

Functional Roles of Group Members/Participants

Roles define patterns of behaviour expected of members. Some roles are officially recognised, and others are termed as informal roles, also known as 'functional roles'. Informal roles are not formally assigned to members. In fact, they are rarely even recognised as existing. Many of the roles may be filled by more than one member, and some of them may be filled by different people at different times.

The informal roles fall into two categories. They are 'task roles' – which help the group accomplish its goals; and 'social roles' – which help the relationships among the members run smoothly. Then there are also dysfunctional roles that prevent a group from working effectively.

Task Roles

- ❑ **Initiator/Contributor** who contributes ideas and suggestions; proposes solutions and decisions.

- **Information seeker** asks for information or facts relevant to the problem and suggests that information is needed before making decisions.
- **Information giver** offers facts or generalisations that may relate to the group's task.
- **Opinion seeker** asks for clarification of opinions made by other members of the group and asks how people in the group feel.
- **Opinion giver** indicates what the group's attitude should be.
- **Elaborator/Clarifier** elaborates ideas and other contributions and offers rationale for the suggestions. Also tries to deduce how an idea or suggestion would work if adopted by the group.
- **Coordinator** clarifies the relationships among information, opinions and ideas.
- **Diagnostician** diagnoses what the problems are.
- **Summarizer** summarizes the whole discussion and raises questions about the direction in which the group is heading.
- **Energizer** simulates the group to act.
- **Procedure developer** handles routine tasks such as seating arrangements, equipments and handing out important papers.
- **Secretary** keps notes on the group's progress.
- **Evaluator/Critic** analyses the group's accomplishments through a criteria and checks to see that consensus has been reached.

Social Roles

- **Supporter/Encourager** praises, agrees with and accepts the contributions of others; offers warmth, solidarity and recognition.
- **Harmonizer** reconciles the disagreements and handles differences. Also reduces tensions by giving group members opportunity to explore their differences.
- **Tension reliever** relaxes the tensed or formal atmosphere through jokes or some other ways.
- **Conciliator** offers new options when his or her own ideas are involved in conflict, willing to admit errors to develop cohesion amongst group members.
- **Gatekeeper** keeps the communication channels open, and encourages the silent members to participate.
- **Follower** goes along with the movement of the group passively accepting the ideas of others, sometimes acting as an audience.

Dysfunctional Roles of Group Members

- **Blocker** interferes with progress by rejecting ideas or taking a negative stand on any and all issues; refuses to cooperate.
- **Aggressor** struggles for status by deflating the status of others through boasting and criticizing.
- **Deserter** withdraws from the discussion and remains aloof and indifferent. Sometimes daydreams and wanders from the subject.
- **Dominator** interrupts on long speeches and monologues, is authoritative and tries to monopolise the group's time.
- **Recognition seeker** usually boasts about past accomplishments and relates irrelevant personal experiences, usually in an attempt to gain sympathy.
- **Joker** displays a lack of involvement in the group through inappropriate humour or cynicism.
- **Cynic** reduces chances of the group's success by portraying a pessimistic outlook.

How to Lead Effective Meetings?

The leader of the meeting has one basic goal – to accomplish the objectives of the meeting. The following guidelines help in leading effective meetings :

- **Starting time:** Start the meeting on time. Nothing says more about the management than starting a meeting at the scheduled time. It also sends the right signals about the level of significance of the concerned meeting and the seriousness of the agenda.
- **Opening remarks:** Establish the right tone – usually serious and positive. Discuss the agenda of the meeting, pointing out some background to the situation and the specific objectives of the meeting.
- **Participation:** It is important to have balanced participation in the meeting from all the members. Effective meetings must ensure that a few members of the group do not dominate the discussion at the expense of their less assertive colleagues. Some direct questions can be asked to the quiet participants.
- **Agenda:** Use the agenda to keep the discussion on track. If the discussion starts to drift from the topic, try to steer it back to the issue. Give a balanced time to each topic listed in the agenda.
- **Closing:** Close the meeting at an appropriate time once the topics in the agenda are covered. Before closing, signal the participants

by asking for any final comments or questions. State a summary of what has been discussed in the meeting. Finally, thank the participants for their time and consideration.

POINTS TO REMEMBER

- A group is formally defined as a small collection of people who interact with each other, usually face to face, over time in order to reach goals.
- A group is more than simply a collection of people and has a distinct personality.
- There can be no denial of the fact that groups are needed – hence, formal groups and informal groups.
- Most groups go through four formative stages group – forming, storming, norming and performing.
- Group communication is defined as the interaction of a group of people to achieve an interdependent goal. Communication facilitates interaction among group members and is an essential process within a group.
- One of the most obvious applications of groups is to solve problems, because groups have the potential to work better than individuals, hence the group decision-making process.
- There are several approaches a group can use to make decisions – consensus, majority control, expert opinion, minority control, authority rule.
- Some commonly used techniques of group problem solving are – brainstorming, nominal group technique, Delphi technique and meetings.
- The very fact that a group has to take decisions requires meeting of group members. Meeting provides a group decision-making forum.
- Meetings have two core purposes – to present information and to help solve problems.
- By meeting procedures, it is implied the procedures adopted to facilitate and record the proceedings of a meeting. The documentation part consists of agenda, notice and minutes and the drafting of resolutions passed in a meeting.
- Certain planning steps and procedures have to be kept in mind before, during and after the meeting.

- Roles define patterns of behaviour expected of members. Some roles are officially recognised, and others are termed as informal roles. The informal roles fall in two categories – task roles and social roles.
- Meetings have one basic goal – to accomplish the objectives of the meeting. Some guidelines help in leading effective meetings.

Chapter

6

Presentation Skills

Learning Objectives

- To understand the importance of business presentations
- To learn how to plan, write and complete a presentation
- Highlighting delivery methods for oral presentations
- To understand some effective ways to grab audience attention
- To understand the importance of visual aids in presentations
- To learn how to create effective slides
- Tips for making effective presentations

The truth isn't the truth until people believe you, and they can't believe you if they don't know what you're saying, and they can't know what you're saying if they don't listen to you, and they won't listen to you if you're not interesting, and you won't be interesting unless you say things imaginatively, originally, freshly.

—William Bernbach

INTRODUCTION

No matter what your area of responsibility is, or the type of organisation for which you work, you will, sooner or later, be expected to give a presentation. It could last 10 minutes or 2 hours. A presentation is a live mode of sharing information with a select audience. In other words, it is a formal talk addressed to one or more people and presents ideas or information in a clear, structured way.

As your career progresses, your presentation skills become more important, because you will be required to depend less on your technical training and more on the ability to sell ideas and plans to their next level of management. Speaking effectively and powerfully is a skill that is really worth learning.

PLANNING A PRESENTATION

- **Study the purpose of your presentation:** The four basic purposes for giving a presentation are: to inform, to persuade, to motivate and to entertain. A presentation is a one time event. You must make sure that the audience hears and remembers what you say. To ensure that, you have to capture their attention and engage them. So the foremost point in preparing your presentation is to begin by defining your purpose clearly and thinking of ways to engage your audience.
  The purpose of your oral presentation will govern the content involved and the style to present the content.
- **Gather needed information:** The relevant information can be gathered and collected through primary and secondary methods.
  - **Primary method:** The primary research (also called field research) involves the collection of data that does not already exist. This can be through numerous forms, including questionnaires and telephone interviews amongst others.
  - **Sceondary method:** The secondary research (also known as desk research) involves the summary, collation and/or synthesis of existing research rather than primary research, where data is collected from research subjects or experiments.
- **Adapt your presentation to occasion and audience:** Establish a good relationship with your audience: to keep your audience members interested in your message, you must understand who your audience members are and what they need. In many cases,

you will be speaking to groups you know little about. Here are some tips on audience analysis :

- **Determine audience size and composition:** Estimate how many people will attend and whether they have something in common – religion, political learning, profession. Try to analyse them on the basis of gender, age ranges, socio-economic groups, occupations, backgrounds.
- **Predict the audience's probable reaction:** Know why they are attending the presentation and their attitude towards the topic – open minded or hostile. Analyse what kind of information they will be more interested in – technical, financial, demonstrations, samples, etc. Don't forget to anticipate possible questions and objections.
- **Gauge their level of understanding:** Analyse whether everybody has same background or experience which will further determine what they already know about the subject. Most importantly, consider whether they are familiar with your vocabulary.
- **Use of the 'you- attitude'** makes your material relevant to your audience and helps keep their attention: people are interested in things that benefit them or affect them personally. Plan to present every point in light of your audience's needs and values.

WRITING A PRESENTATION

- **Define the main idea:** What is the one message that you want your audience members to remember after your presentation? The main idea points out how the audience can benefit from your message. For example, if you are giving a sales presentation, focus on the benefits of the product to the audience rather than how great the product is.
- **Time frame:** You must tailor to the time allowed which is often regulated. Hence you need to present the important points in the first few minutes. Always remember: never squeeze a complex presentation into a period too short, and never spend unnecessary time on a simple talk.
- **Decide on an appropriate style:** If you are speaking to a small group, you can use a casual style that encourages audience participation. Use simple visual aids and deliver in a conversational tone. If you are addressing a large audience, a

formal atmosphere needs to be established. These presentations are often done with slides and other visual aids.

- To complete your oral presentations, you need to **revise and proofread** the message for clarity and conciseness.

MASTERING THE ART OF DELIVERY

After the planning and writing of an oral presentation, the delivery of the message should be taken care of. Be thoroughly familiar with your subject and always use familiar language. There are various delivery methods.

- Reading
- Memorising
- Speaking from notes
- Impromptu Speaking

OVERCOMING STAGE FRIGHT AND FEELING MORE CONFIDENT

It is not only first time speakers or amateurs who feel stage fright, but even experienced speakers feel some anxiety about getting up in front of an audience. You are suffering from stage fright if you have trembling lips, tight throat, dry mouth, sweaty and cold hands, nausea, and wobbly knees. Some effective tips to feel more confident are :

- Concentrate on how good you are and try to feel as if you are chatting with your friends.
- Be extremely well-prepared, anticipate all possible questions, rehearse and prepare more material than necessary.
- Be in the room at least half an hour early so as to check everything. Visualise your success and be comfortable. Think positively.
- When the presentation begins, use eye contact. Look at friendly and warm faces and don't comment or mention your nervousness. Take a few deep breaths and don't panic.

HANDLING QUESTIONS RESPONSIVELY

The question-answer round is the most critical aspect of a presentation. Try to keep these handy tips in mind while answering the questions :

- **Focus on the questioner and respond appropriately:** Orient your whole body language in such a way that your complete attention is targeted towards the questioner. Nod your head to acknowledge the question and repeat it to confirm your understanding.

Be sure to answer the question. Don't ignore or laugh it off. If you don't know the answer, don't pretend you do. Remember, you don't have to answer every question that is asked.

- **Maintain control:** Establish some ground rules so as to avoid heated arguments. Establish some timeframe and regulations for asking questions. Don't let one or two people monopolise the question period. Give as many audience members as possible a chance to participate by calling on people from different parts of the room.

SOME EFFECTIVE WAYS TO GRAB AUDIENCE ATTENTION

No matter how experienced and effective a presenter you are, or how important your topic is, you can quickly lose an audience if you do not grab their attention and arouse interest. You have to sound interesting and set the right tone. Most importantly, an attention getter should create curiosity in the minds of the listeners, and convince them that the talk will be interesting and useful.

Some popular ways to grab the attention of the audience are given below. You may use those which suit the topic.

- **Telling a Story:** Stories are naturally interesting and compelling. Most people enjoy a good story. Be sure your story illustrates an important point.
- **Asking questions:** Rhetorical questions are designed to arouse curiosity without requiring an answer. Asking questions will get the audience actively involved in your presentation
- **Quotations:** Stating quotations from a famous person can prove to be interesting. The quotations compel the audience to focus on your topic.
- **Use humour:** Although business presentations are meant to be serious business, a light and humourous remark can perk up the audience. It also helps people relax and lighten the atmosphere. Just be sure that the humour is relevant and not offensive.
- **Giving samples:** The best way to make people remember your presentation is by appealing to their senses. What better way than to give them samples!
- **Startling statements:** People tend to focus on that which is unique and amazing. Startling statements or events, shocking facts, and interesting statistics are effective for grabbing audience attention.

USING VISUAL AIDS IN ORAL PRESENTATIONS

Good content and smooth delivery are not enough in an oral presentation. Visual aids can improve the quality and impact of your presentation by creating interest, illustrating points that are difficult to explain in words, adding variety, and increasing the audience's ability to absorb and remember important points.

Visual aids also help the speaker remember important details and improve his/her professional image also.

Speakers have a variety of visual aids to choose from. Some of the more popular are given below :

1. **Overhead Transparencies:** It is a piece of clear plastic with writing or some image on it. Transparencies are shown by placing them on an overhead projector that projects the material on screen. They can be prepared by using software or by hand.
   The advantages are numerous. They are inexpensive, easy to create and simple to use. They require little extra equipment as most classrooms usually have overhead projectors. Speakers can also maintain eye contact with their audience, because the images can be projected in full daylight.
   They also have a few disadvantages. They must be replaced if their content changes; one cannot change or erase anything on a transparency. Moreover, they are prone to scratches and tear easily. They are difficult to modify and clumsy to use.
2. **Electronic presentations:** It is also known as 'slide show' which is composed using popular computer software such as Microsoft Power point. The software allows you to incorporate photos, sound, video, graphics, animation, and other movement into the slides, enabling the speaker to capture and engage the audience like no other visual aid. For live presentations, LCD (liquid crystal display) projectors or display panels are used.
   The biggest advantage of slides is their computerised format; one can change and edit the material as per convenience. One can add animations, video clips, sound, hyperlinks and other multimedia effects to make the presentation more effective. They are easy to store, transport and can be customised for different audiences.
   The disadvantages are: Firstly, electronic slides require expensive display equipment. The equipment is complicated to use and may not be available in all situations. Secondly, people

tend to spend too much time on the animation and special effects of their slide shows rather than on the content.

3. **Chalkboards and whiteboards:** They are effective tools for recording points in small group sessions. They are produced on the spot and offer flexibility. However, they are too informal for some situations.
4. **Flip charts:** Large sheets of paper are attached at the top of an easel so that you can flip the pages as you speak, with each chart illustrating a point.
5. **Other Visual aids:** Audiotapes are often used to supplement a slide show. Filmstrips and movies are effective tools to capture the audience's attention. Television and videotapes are good for showing demonstrations, interviews and other events. Models built to scale are convenient representations of an object. Moreover, sample of a product or material allows the audience to experience the topic directly.

CREATING EFFECTIVE SLIDES

People cannot read and listen at the same time, so the slides must be simple enough for the audience to understand within a moment or two.

Readable: One of the biggest mistakes while making slides is to overload them with too much information. Text slides are not there to display your entire script or highlight each point you make. They are not your notes. Slides with excessive text take the audience's eyes off the speaker.

- Slides with too much text, long sentences, or bullets are difficult to read from a distance and difficult to understand. They confuse and distract the audience.
- When writing content for slides, keep it short and simple.
- Limit each slide to one thought, concept or idea.
- Write in bullets rather than long sentences.
- Include short informative titles.

Design elements: Design is an important element of presentations. It transforms a dull presentation into something dynamic and readable. Once you have decided and selected the best design elements for your slides, stick to them and be consistent.

- **Colour:** It is a critical design element. It can make your slides attractive, lively and professional. It also plays an important role in the overall acceptance of your message. It can increase willingness to read, enhance learning and improve retention. For example, if you wish to stimulate and excite your audience, use colours like red and orange; similarly if you want to relax them, use blue.

Keep in mind that contrasting colours increase readability. So when selecting backgrounds, titles and texts, avoid choosing colours that are close in type – yellow text on a white background, brown on green, blue on black and purple, etc. Use blue which is generally considered safe and conservative. When changing slides, don't switch colours, as it would be harsh to the audience eyes.

- **Background:** A good background design is critical to an effective presentation. Custom designs usually include a company logo and company colours. Many companies also hire professional graphic designers and make purchases from Internet or use other software packages. Choose a background design that is simple, relevant to the subject and appeals to the audience. Avoid ones dominated by heavy colour, busy patterns or strong graphics.
- **Clip art:** Try avoiding the use of inappropriate, oversized or unnecessary clip arts which distract the audience from the message. Make sure it completely fits the slide's overall design. Don't use something just because you have it or are tempted to use it.
- **Fonts and type styles:** Avoid decorative fonts. Limit your fonts – reserve one for headings, other for bulleted points. Avoid the italicised type as it hampers reading. Headings of the same level should use the same font, type size and colour.
- **Hyperlink:** When you click on a slide's hyperlink, you are immediately transported to a different file stored in your computer or even to a webpage. They allow building interactivity and prove to be a great tool, without having to incorporate each detail into a slide.

TIPS FOR MAKING EFFECTIVE PRESENTATIONS

In any successful oral presentation, getting your message across to an audience requires clear communication.

- **Speak slowly and clearly:** Articulate every word carefully. Emphasise for clarity and pause frequently so that the audience will have time to absorb the information. Don't speak too fast thereby making the matter incomprehensible to the listener.

Similarly, don't speak too slow thereby making the speech boring and dull.

- **Repeat key words and phrases:** Sometimes audiences need to hear important information more than once. When audiences are not familiar with your language, try to use the same words for repetition. For example, if you have used the word 'advantages', then don't use the word 'benefits' again.
- **Keep your message simple and clear:** Eliminate complex sentence structure, acronyms, and abbreviations. Stay away from idioms which may confuse the audience.
- **Communicate with non-verbal language:** Your verbal message should be accompanied with non-verbal language. Establish a relationship with your audience through an eye contact. Moreover, don't forget to smile. Your physical appearance, dressing and personal grooming will also play an important role in making your presentation successful.
- **Support your message with visual aids:** Always remember that a picture is worth a thousand words. Visual messages support and clarify spoken messages. Handouts, graphs, pictorial presentations, overheads and electronic PowerPoint slides can make your message effective.
- Lastly and most importantly, **being yourself**, having fun and letting your personality shine through are some of the ways speakers can create a lasting impression on their audience.

POINTS TO REMEMBER

- A presentation is a live mode of sharing information with a select audience.
- Planning a presentation involves studying of purpose and audience, gathering relevant information, and adapting the presentation to audience and occasion.
- Writing a presentation involves defining the main idea, keeping a timeframe, choosing an approach, and an appropriate style.
- Completing a presentation would include revising and proofreading for conciseness and clarity.
- There are various delivery methods to choose from while preparing for a presentation.
- Overcoming stage fright and feeling more confident is the key to an effective presentation.

- The question-answer round is the most critical aspect of a presentation. Keeping in mind some handy tips will help in answering the questions responsively.
- No matter how experienced and effective a presenter you are, or how important your topic is, you can quickly lose an audience if you don't grab their attention and arouse interest.
- Visual aids helps improve the quality and impact of your presentation by creating interest, illustrating points that are difficult to explain in words, adding variety and increasing the audience's ability to absorb and remember important points.
- People cannot read and listen at the same time, so the slides must be simple enough for the audience to understand within a moment or two.
- In any successful oral presentation, getting your message across to an audience requires clear communication.

Chapter

7

Business Etiquette

Learning Objectives

- Understanding the concept and importance of etiquette in business communication
- Understanding the general rules of business etiquette
- Learning ways to deal with superiors, peers and subordinates
- Learning how to interact with foreign clients
- Learning how to handle meetings and phone calls
- Learning the nuances of e-mail etiquette
- Learning to deal with interruptions
- Learning how to interact with guests, consultants and new employees
- Understanding the importance of dress/appearance in business etiquette
- Learning ways of introducing
- Learning table manners

Evil communication corrupts good manners? I hope to live to hear that good communication corrects bad manners.

—Benjamin Banneker

INTRODUCTION

Business etiquette is made up of significantly more important things than knowing which fork to use at lunch with a client. Etiquette is about presenting yourself with the kind of polish that shows you can be taken seriously. Etiquette is also about being comfortable around people (and making them comfortable around you!).

People are a key factor in your own and your business' success. Many potentially worthwhile and profitable alliances have been lost because of an unintentional breach of manners.

Most behaviour that is perceived as disrespectful, discourteous or abrasive is unintentional, and could have been avoided by practicing good manners or etiquette. We have always found that most negative experiences with someone were unintentional and easily repaired by keeping an open mind and maintaining open, honest communication. Basic knowledge and practise of etiquette is a valuable advantage, because in a lot of situations, a second chance may not be possible or practical.

There are many written and unwritten rules and guidelines for etiquette. These guidelines have some difficult-to-navigate nuances, depending on the company, the local culture, and the requirements of the situation. Possibilities to commit *a faux pas* are limitless, and chances are, sooner or later, you will make a mistake. But you can minimise them, recover quickly, and avoid causing a bad impression by being generally considerate and attentive to the concerns of others, and by adhering to the basic rules of etiquette. When in doubt, stick to the basics.

THE BASICS

The most important thing to remember is to be courteous and thoughtful to the people around you, regardless of the situation. Consider other people's feelings, stick to your convictions as diplomatically as possible. Address conflict as situation-related, rather than person-related.

Avoid raising your voice (surprisingly, it can be much more effective at getting attention!), using harsh or derogatory language toward anyone (present or absent), or interrupting. You may not get as much 'airtime' in meetings at first, but what you do say will be much more effective because it carries the weight of credibility and respectability.

The following are guidelines and tips that are helpful for dealing with people in general, in work environments, and in social situations.

IT'S ALL ABOUT PEOPLE

Talk and visit with people. Don't differentiate by position or standing within the company. Secretaries and janitorial staff actually have tremendous power to help or hinder your career. Next time you need a document prepared or a conference room arranged for a presentation, watch how many people are involved with that process (you will probably be surprised!) and make it a point to meet them and show your appreciation.

Make it a point to arrive ten or fifteen minutes early and visit with people that work near you. When you are visiting another site, linger over a cup of coffee and introduce yourself to people nearby. If you arrive early for a meeting, introduce yourself to the other participants. At social occasions, use the circumstances of the event itself as an icebreaker. Talk a little about yourself – your hobbies, kids, or pets; just enough to get people to open up about theirs and get to know you as a person.

Keep notes on people. They help you create a 'people database' with names, addresses, phone numbers, birthdays, spouse and children's' names; whatever depth of information is appropriate for your situation.

It is a good idea to remember what you can about people; and to be thoughtful. Send cards or letters for birthdays or congratulations of promotions or other events; send flowers for engagements, weddings or in condolence for the death of a loved one or family member. People will remember your kindness, probably much longer than you will!

Peers and Subordinates

Impressing the boss is not enough..!

Experts are of the opinion that a majority of new management employees fail in their first jobs. The key reason for their failure is their inability to build good relationships with peers and subordinates.

Most people believe that it is more important to show respect and practise etiquette around superiors than around peers or subordinates. However, the current social and economic climate is one of rapid advancement through technology, which makes it very possible (and even likely) for a salesman to become an important client, or an administrative assistant to become a manager. Mergers and acquisitions add to this 'class mixing', causing a former competitor to become a coworker overnight. This can make things awkward if you treat people differently depending on their 'corporate standing'. If you show respect and courtesy to everyone, regardless of position or company, you avoid discomfort or damaging your chances in any unexpected turn of events.

Having a consistent demeanor improves your credibility. Even the people at the top will begin to suspect your motives if you treat VIPs with impeccable courtesy and snap at counter clerks.

Superiors

The only thing you owe your boss above and beyond what you owe peers and subordinates is more information. Unobtrusively be sure he or she knows what you are doing, is alerted as early as possible to issues that may arise, and is aware of outcomes and milestones.

Never surprise your boss.

It goes without saying that you should speak well of him or her within and outside the company.

INTERCULTURAL BUSINESS

It is important to note that etiquette in other cultures requires a bit of adaptation and flexibility. If you are travelling on business to a foreign destination, or have visitors here, it is a good idea to learn as much as you can about the culture they are coming from and make appropriate allowances. You may consider the following :

- Language (make an effort to learn theirs if possible, but don't pretend to be fluent unless you have many years of study under your belt!)
- Time zones
- Working schedules
- Holidays
- Food customs (table manners, use of implements, etc.)

Generally speaking, as long as you are trying to be considerate and express an interest in learning, you should be fine. If in doubt, err on the conservative, formal side.

MEETINGS

If a subject is important enough to call a meeting, be considerate of the participants' time and ensure that you are well-prepared.

Communicate beforehand

- the objective
- the expected duration (be sure to observe the ending time scrupulously, unless everyone agrees to continue)
- items expected to be discussed.

Often overlooked – be sure to 'thank' meeting members for their time and participation, and demonstrate (in the minutes or written record, at least) how their contributions helped meet the objective of the meeting. Participants are frequently left wondering if they have been heard or if their attendance and contributions were noticed. Distribute minutes or some written record (no matter how simple the meeting) to all attendees and absentees, with concise but complete descriptions of decisions made and including action items.

PHONE CALLS

Always return calls. Even if you do not yet have an answer to the caller's question, call and explain what you are doing to get the requested information, or direct them to the appropriate place to get it.

If you are going to be out, have someone pick up your calls or, at a minimum, have your answering system tell the caller when you will be back in the office and when they can expect a call back.

When you initiate a call and get a receptionist or secretary, identify yourself and tell them the basic nature of your call. That way, you will be sure you are getting the right person or department and the person you are trying to reach will be able to pull up the appropriate information and help you more efficiently.

When you are on the receiving end of a phone call, identify yourself and your department. Answer the phone with some enthusiasm or at least warmth, even if you are being interrupted, after all the person on the other end does not know that!

Make sure your voice mail system is working properly and does not tell the caller that the mailbox is full, transfer them to nowhere, or ring indefinitely. Address technical and system problems – a rude machine or system is as unacceptable as a rude person.

You do not have to reply to obvious solicitations. If someone is calling to sell you something, you can indicate that you are not interested and hang up without losing too much time on it. However, you do need to be careful. You may be receiving a call from an insurance or long distance company that wants to hire you as a consultant! Be sure you know the nature of the call before you (politely, of course) excuse yourself.

And always remember to smile when talking on phone – the person at the other can sense it!

E-MAIL

Make the subject line specific. Think of the many messages you have received with the generic subject line, 'Hi' or 'Just for you'.

When replying to a question, copy only the question into your e-mail, then provide your response. You need not hit reply automatically, but don't send a bare message that only reads, 'Yes'. It's too blunt and confuses the reader.

Address and sign your e-mails. Although this is included in the To and From sections, remember that you're communicating with a person, not a computer.

DON'T TYPE IN ALL CAPS. It's too intense, and you appear too lazy to type properly. This is still a written medium. Follow standard writing guidelines as a professional courtesy.

INTERRUPTIONS

Avoid interruptions (of singular or group work sessions, meetings, phone calls, or even discussions) if at all possible. Most management folks feel free to interrupt informal working sessions of subordinates, but need to realise that they may be interrupting a brainstorming session that will produce the company's next big success.

Always apologise if you must interrupt a conversation, meeting, or someone's concentration on a task. Quickly state the nature of what you need, and show consideration for the fact that you are interrupting valuable work or progress.

GUESTS, CONSULTANTS AND NEW EMPLOYEES

If you have a new employee, guest, or consultant working at your company for a day, week, or longer, be sure that that person has the resources and information that he or she needs to do the job. This is not just courtesy, it is good business sense, since time spent flailing around looking for things is embarrassing to the consultant and expensive for your company.

Give a consultant or guest the same type of workspace as an employee at your company in a similar role. A consultant who is there to do programming should have, if at all possible, the same size cube, type of computer equipment, etc. as an employee programmer would have in your company. This prevents your employees from feeling looked down-upon, and the consultant from feeling singled out or treated as second-rate.

A guest from a regulatory agency will tend to want to know what's 'really' going on in the company. By treating him or her like everyone else (instead of isolating them in a plush office in a far wing, for example) will raise less suspicion and enable them to get the information they need more efficiently.

Appoint an employee to be a 'buddy' to a guest or consultant to ensure that they are introduced around, 'shown the ropes', and have someone to help resolve little logistical problems that may arise and cause non-productivity or embarrassment.

APPRECIATION AND CREDIT

Always pass along credit and compliments to everyone who made a contribution to the effort. Speak well of your coworkers and always point out their accomplishments to any interested party. Appearing to have taken the credit in superiors' or customers' eyes is the surest way to sabotage a relationship with a coworker.

DRESS/APPEARANCE

It can be insulting to your coworkers or clients if you show a lack of concern about your appearance.

Being wrinkled, unshaven, smelly or unkempt communicates (intentionally or not) that you do not care enough about the situation, the people, or the company to present yourself respectably.

If in doubt, always err on the side of conservative. Women's clothing is a bit more complicated, but again, err on the side of conservative and dressy.

Always practise impeccable grooming (even in a jeans environment!).

Aim to have three great outfits. These should be good quality, conservative, clean, and in good repair. Clothes should fit right; they should neither be figure hugging nor too loose. Buy clothes that suit your body type and complement your body. Of course, you'll also need.

- Clean and polished dress shoes
- A well-groomed hairstyle
- Cleaned and trimmed fingernails
- And, of course, you should be clean and well-groomed yourself.

For Men

- Conservative dark navy or grey two-piece business suit (if you have only one or two suits, make sure you make some differences with your tie or shirt in subsequent interviews)
- A white long-sleeved button-down dress shirt
- A conservative silk tie
- Clean, well-polished dress shoes

For Women

- Pick a conservative colour such as dark blue, dark grey, brown, cream, or beige.
- Steer clear of sleeveless and transparent tops.
- For business/corporate situations, match your handbag, shoes and belts. Shoes should be matched with the handbag.
- The classic suit should be a wardrobe staple. Jackets can be worn with skirts and pants. Skirts should be no shorter than four inches above the knee.
- Steer clear of your favourite sandals, disco boots, mini skirts and tattered jeans.
- Choose a good quality leather belt and don't wear flashy or plastic belts. If you don't like wearing belts, then steer clear from pants with loops.
- Make-up and perfume should be in good taste. Avoid visible body piercing, only pierced ears are acceptable (in some countries, pierced nose is also acceptable).
- Shoes should be clean, well-polished and in good repair, with closed toes and low heels.

SOCIAL SETTINGS

Many impressions formed during a party, dinner or golf game can make or break a key business arrangement, whether or not business is discussed directly. Always carry business cards. Arrive at a party at the stated time or up to 30 minutes later (not earlier than the stated time, under any circumstances).

Introductions

Before an event, use your address book or your 'people database' to refresh your memory about the people you are likely to meet.

If you forget someone's name, you can sometimes 'cover' by introducing a person you do know first. 'Do you know Mr Ankur Mehta, one of our accounts representatives?' which will usually get the unknown person to introduce himself.

If this does not work, an admission that you have had a mental block is preferable to obvious flailing around.

Table Manners

Many 'getting to know you' encounters take place over a meal. Sharing a meal is a time-honoured tradition of hospitality, and a great way to get to know a person. Whether this is your first encounter with the prospective employer, recruiter, or other contact, having good table manners is imperative.

- ❑ Remember that eating is your secondary objective. Making a good impression on your dining partners is your primary objective. Concentrate more on the conversation than the food.
- ❑ Your water/beverages are on the right, bread is on your left.
- ❑ Don't 'reach' – ask for items to be passed.
- ❑ Don't smoke or drink alcohol, unless everyone else at the table is doing so. Even then, practice extreme moderation.
- ❑ Utensils, once used, should never again touch the table. Rest them on a saucer or plate.

Here is what you should keep in mind at a formal dinner.

1. Do one thing at a time. If you want to sip your wine, temporarily rest your fork or knife on the plate.
2. What to do if the table is improperly set? Don't rearrange an improperly arranged place setting as it may offend the hostess.
3. Where to place the hands while eating: To avoid creating obstruction to your dinner partner, when holding a utensil, rest your other hand in your lap. When not holding any utensils, both hands remain in the lap.
4. Resist the urge to create a relaxed ambience, to fidget, to rearrange silverware, twist the linens, drum on the table, and play with salt and pepper shakers. For cleanliness, keep hands away from face and hair.
5. Good posture at the table means sitting straight with the back rested slightly against the back of the chair. To avoid spills, lean over the plate each time you take a bite. Avoid wrapping your feet around the legs of the chair. Refrain from leaning back and extending your legs under the table, or putting your arm on the back of the dinner partner's chair.
6. Elbows and forearms should remain off the table. To avoid crowding one's dinner partner during a meal, the elbows remain close to the body and off the table. To prevent a barrier to conversation, the forearm and hand are not wrapped around the plate. But, sometimes in crowded and noisy places, elbows are rested on the table so one may lean forward to listen.
7. When food that you don't like or can't eat is served, take a small portion of it, rather than making an issue out of it and offending

your host. Place the portion on the plate, dabble with it, and eat a small amount (or none at all!). To compensate, take larger portions of other foods. In case of allergy, say 'No, thank you' and after the meal, quietly explain to the host. At a buffet, take only the foods you like.

8. When a guest spills food at a formal dinner, the butler takes the appropriate action. At an informal dinner, the guest quietly and quickly lifts the food with a utensil and places it on the side of his/her plate.
9. How large a portion to take from a platter. When a platter of pre-sliced food is presented, and each size is ample, take one serving. But if the slices are small, and there are enough servings for each guest to have two, take two for yourself. As a courtesy to the last guest, make sure to leave enough food on the platter.
10. To refuse a beverage, do not wave hands or cover up a glass or turn cup upside down, simply say, 'No, thank you'.

The important thing to remember is that if you strive to make the people around you feel comfortable and valued, you have succeeded whether or not you are perfectly in compliance with these or any rules you have read.

POINTS TO REMEMBER

- Etiquette is about presenting yourself with the kind of polish that shows you can be taken seriously.
- The most important thing to remember is to be courteous and thoughtful to the people around you, regardless of the situation.
- The ability to build good relationships with peers and subordinates accounts for a major portion of success in jobs.
- You should speak well of your boss within and outside the company.
- Etiquette in other cultures requires a bit of adaptation and flexibility.
- If a subject is important enough to call a meeting, be considerate of the participants' time and ensure that you are well-prepared.
- Certain telephone etiquette have to be borne in mind – returning back the call, ensuring your voice mail system is working, and not forgetting to smile when talking on phone – to ensure a long lasting relationship with people.
- Certain e-mail etiquette should be adopted to ensure professionalism.

- Avoid interruptions (of singular or group work sessions, meetings, phone calls, or even discussions) if at all possible.
- If you have a new employee, guest, or consultant working at your company for a day, week, or longer, be sure that that person has the resources and information that he or she needs to do the job.
- Always pass along credit and compliments to everyone who made a contribution to the effort.
- Always practise impeccable grooming.
- Before an event, use your address book or your 'people database' to refresh your memory about the people you are likely to meet.
- Sharing a meal is a time-honoured tradition of hospitality, and a great way to get to know a person. Whether this is your first encounter with the prospective employer, recruiter, or other contact, having good table manners is imperative.

Chapter

8

Business Ethics

Learning Objectives

- To know the concept and nature of ethics
- To know the characteristics of ethical communication
- To understand the guidelines for spoken and written messages
- To understand the guidelines for cross-cultural messages
- To understand the guidelines for advertising
- To understand what influences personal ethics

Whenever two good people argue over principles, they are both right.

—Marie Ebner Von Eschenbach

WHAT ARE ETHICS?

Ethics are the principles of conduct that govern a person or a group. Unethical people say or do whatever it takes to achieve their end. Ethical people are generally trustworthy, fair and impartial, respecting the rights of others and are concerned about the impact of their actions on society. Ethics is aptly defined as 'knowing the difference between what you have a right to do and what is the right thing to do'.

Ethics is about making right and wrong decisions. Ethical principles assist in making those decisions and help to communicate effectively. These principles centre on fairness, service, quality, integrity, excellence, compassion, honesty and dignity.

We communicate our values and beliefs to others via verbal and non-verbal behaviour. We are defined in the eyes of others according to the way we behave. Subsequently, we have a responsibility to act in ways that promote honesty and fairness so that the personal worth of each person in the organisation can be maximised. There is also the need to communicate the importance and necessity of good ethics to others.

Ethical issues are those that focus on value judgments concerning right and wrong, goodness and badness in human conduct. Ethics go beyond questions of legality or illegality. The field of ethics considers what our relationships are, and ought to be, with our employers, employees, colleagues, subordinates, customers, stockholders, suppliers and distributors, and other members of the community in which we operate.

At the foundation of ethical behaviour is a value system. Values are the most stable and enduring characteristics of individuals, and are the basis upon which attitudes and personal preferences are formed, involving crucial decisions, life direction and personal tastes.

Organisations also have value systems. Managers at all levels are stressing on integrity and competence. Successful companies have clearly stated values that make sense to their employees, and they reinforce these values through everything they do.

ETHICAL COMMUNICATION

An ethical message is accurate and sincere. It avoids language that manipulates, discriminates, or exaggerates. When communicating ethically, you do not hide negative information behind an optimistic attitude; you do not state opinions as facts and portray graphic data fairly. You are honest with employers, co-workers and clients, never seeking gain by making others look better or worse than they are. You do not allow personal preferences to influence your perception or the perception of others, and you act in good faith.

From a communication point of view, ethical communication helps the individual's ability to make sound choices. Ethical communication may include providing complete and accurate information upon which others can base their choices.

Some important characteristics of ethical communication are as follows :

- Maintaining a long lasting relationship with the audience
- Getting the message across without offending anyone
- Being non-judgmental and non-evaluative
- Presenting information without holding back any key points or vital information
- Being empathic, thereby seeing issues and problems from other's perspectives, and identifying with other's needs, values and interests
- Making sure all information is accurate and well-researched
- Willing to admit that one could be wrong and being open to new ideas thereby adopting a flexible and open approach
- Maintaining an honest approach. Individuals and organisations should avoid falsehoods, deceptive statements or incorrect conclusions or data.
- One ought to be sensitive to cultural differences. In a global setting, there are multiple cultures to accommodate, which leaves room for multiple sets of rules and expectations to apply.

The modern global world, with its large-scale operations, has led to an increased interest in values and principles that provide a platform for decision-making. The study of ethics in communication represents such a platform. Communication is linked to ethics through the common principles of truth and honesty, trust and relationships, reputation and integrity, conduct and justice.

UNETHICAL COMMUNICATION

Ethical communication includes all relevant information which is true in every sense and is not deceptive in any way. By contrast, unethical communication can include falsehoods and misleading information, or withholding important information. Some instances of unethical communication include :

- **Plagiarism:** Stealing somebody's words or work and claiming it as your own. Also known as stealing the intellectual property of others.

- **Selective misquoting:** Deliberately omitting or damaging negative information to present a better, but untruthful picture of you or the company.
- **Misrepresenting numbers:** Altering the numerical and statistical data.
- **Distorting visuals:** Distorting the graphics, or changing the scale of graphs and charts to exaggerate or conceal differences.

KEY AREAS FOR ETHICAL COMMUNICATION

Ethical treatment of a subject takes time, thought and preparation. As a manager, it is imperative to focus on ethical communication in three key areas: the written and spoken messages, cross-cultural messages, and the advertising that the company creates. These areas are important because work nowadays is becoming increasingly global, and sensitivity to diversity is now an important managerial skill.

Ethical Guidelines for Spoken and Written Messages

1. **Research methods:** The individual has to doubly ensure that the sources are contemporary, reliable and impartial.
2. **Purpose:** When the purpose is fulfilled, it should benefit the audience. One also has to introspect whether one has any hidden agendas that affect the purpose.
3. **Selection of material:** The material should be chosen in such a manner that it communicates the ideas fairly and accurately. The sources should be representative of the information available on the topic.
4. **Development of ideas:** The logic and reasoning should be sound and should not rely heavily on emotional appeals. The propaganda techniques that omit, exaggerate or distort information should be avoided. The information should be accurate and relevant.
5. **Use of language:** Familiar language should be used. Jargons should be completely avoided. The language should not be vague, ambiguous, abstract. Most importantly, it should show respect for listeners and be concrete and specific.
6. **Ethical perspective:** The audience's feelings, values and attitudes should be considered. A 'you-attitude' should be adopted.

Ethical Guidelines for Cross-Cultural Messages

1. **Cultural context:** The feelings, values and opinions of the individual from the other culture should be kept in mind. Attempts should be made to understand the context of operation from the other person's position and situation.
2. **Language:** Familiar and universally accepted vocabulary should be used. Use language that can be clearly understood by others. Take care not to use language and expressions that humiliate and are offensive to the other cultures. Be aware of the non-verbal aspects of your message, and in what context they are being understood by the other person, and how it changes the entire meaning of the content.
3. **Misunderstandings:** Try to anticipate and correct any probable misunderstandings that might occur.
4. **Accountability:** Fulfill the standard for cross-cultural ethics. Be fair and just to everyone involved.

Ethical Guidelines for Advertising

1. **Language:** Represent the product or event using clear, straightforward language. Take care not to make exaggerations and be truthful in your approach. Ensure that the product can be taken on face value.
2. **Graphics:** Ensure that the product is accurately depicted through the graphics in the advertising. Significant information should be highlighted making the viewer see it easily.
3. **Omission:** Key details that may affect the customer's views regarding the product should not be omitted. Significant information should not be unstated which might change the customer's perception of the product, if this information were included.
4. **Truth:** The product or the event should fulfill the expectations it has created.
5. **Accountability:** The company should be ready and comfortable if the advertising techniques be scrutinised by some authority and also be printed for the public to read. It should also be open to the idea of meeting face to face the consumers who have bought the product.

Ethical issues are bound to come up because communication plays a significant role in influencing others. The way a person communicates in the organisation is largely affected by the way he or she wants to be perceived by others, and also how he or she would like others to behave.

Ethics is often a communication issue. Your employees and colleagues learn about your ethics and values by observing your actions. Modelling ethical behaviour is an important managerial tool.

PERSONAL ETHICS

Your family and peers, culture and philosophy influence your personal ethics. Managers need to be aware of these influences.

- **People:** Your family members and friends exert a strong influence on your ethics. Parents and other family members play a key role in shaping the value system early on, which tends to stay with us throughout our lives. Your parents have left an imprint of what is right and wrong in your mind.
  Teachers also play an effective role in shaping value systems. Peers also influence the ethics and, finally, in life you choose to be close to people who share your own value system.
- **Culture:** Culture teaches certain ethical values. People who grow up in cities have a different value system as compared to those who have grown up in small towns. Similarly, people of different countries also have different values and ethics. Each culture, over time, acquires its own set of values.
- **Philosophy:** Theories of philosophy have long been concerned with ethical and moral issues. Your actions in a situation depend on which philosophical perspective reflects your personal beliefs.
- **Law:** Some individuals view ethics from a legal perspective – they feel acting ethically means following the law.
- **Religion:** Religions serve as a major foundation for ethical behaviour among its followers. Using religion as the grounding for your ethical behaviour means you act according to what God wants you to do.

ETHICAL CHOICES

Every organisation has responsibilities to various groups: customers, employees, share-holders, suppliers and so on. What may be a right decision for one may be wrong for another. Sometimes one is presented with an option that seems right on the surface but is somewhere wrong.

Conflicting priorities and the grey areas between right and wrong create ethical dilemmas for an organisation's communicators. An ethical dilemma involves choosing alternatives that are not clear, that is, they fall under the blurring lines of right and wrong.

While making ethical choices, laws provide ethical guidelines for certain type of messages. However, very often, one has to depend on one's own judgment and principles. Self-introspection can sometimes help you decide as to what is ethical.

Modern businesses foster ethical behaviour by using a written code of ethics to help employees determine what is acceptable. Moreover, setting a good ethical example is contagious, as others will follow your conduct and see the success you experience both in your interpersonal relationships and career.

POINTS TO REMEMBER

- Ethics is about making right and wrong decisions. Ethical principles assist in making those decisions and help to communicate effectively.
- From a communication point of view, ethical communication helps the individual's ability to make sound choices.
- Studying of important characteristics of ethical communication forms a platform for sound decision-making.
- A manager must know the ethical guidelines for preparing written and spoken messages, cross-cultural messages, advertising messages.
- Managers need to be aware of the influences that shape personal ethics.

Chapter

9

Impact of IT on Communication

Learning Objectives

- To understand the concept and importance of information technology in business communication
- To understand the various types of technologies available for business communication
- To learn e-mail etiquette
- To know the positive impacts of technology on business communication
- To know the negative impacts of technology on business communication

The newest computer can merely compound, at speed, the oldest problem in the relations between human beings, and in the end the communication will be confronted with the old problem, of what to say and how to say it.

—Edward R. Murrow

INTRODUCTION

In this 'age of communication', you are considered wealthy if you have information about and wide access to different means of communication. Technologies such as the Internet, e-mail, voice mail, video conferencing and faxes allow people from all parts of the world to work together around the globe 24 hours a day. Technological tools can enhance the uniquely human ability to communicate. But as with any set of tools, how one uses them determines their degree of effectiveness.

Appropriately used, technology can assist individuals and organisations with the work related to writing as well as the creative, thinking aspects. Technology has an ever- increasing presence in the work place. More and more businesses, large and small, are trying to incorporate the latest technology into their operations. It is revolutionising the way organisations communicate.

The use of communication technology can tackle some of the basic problems, namely, accuracy, speed, cost, quality, quantity in the light of wide corporate business operations. The pre-dominant method of communication in many organisations has been through old and manual methods which are expensive, take time, lack accuracy, and are unable to shoulder a large quantity of messages.

So, search for alternative methods has become imperative in the modern complex business organisations, where messages have to be communicated across vast geographical territory, both inside and outside the country.

When entering the corporate world, individuals will be expected to know how to use modern technologies for effective workplace communication. The various technology based communication tools used in organisations for acquiring, transmitting and processing information are discussed below.

INTERNET

The internet is the world's largest computer network. It is accessible to individuals, companies, colleges, government agencies and other institutions all over the world. It links thousands of smaller computer networks and millions of individual computer users in homes, businesses and offices worldwide. It can be used at a basic level for e- mail and for research, and it can be used at a more comprehensive level as a channel for selling products and services.

To reach the internet, one needs a computer with a modem and an Internet service provider (ISP) – a company that provides access to the internet. The most widely used part of internet is the world wide web.

Internet is so easy to navigate that businesses are using it to make closer connections with organisations and customers all over the planet. More importantly, it has changed the way companies operate internally by allowing speedy, convenient exchanges of ideas and information.

All the uses of internet have one thing in common – they improve communication, which is the most important advantage that managers get.

E-MAIL

Electronic mail (e-mail) enables users to create, send and read written messages entirely on computer. An e-mail document may be a simple text message, or it might include complex files or programs. Electronic communication is so quick and easy that it is often the most popular way to contact people. Sending e-mail almost guarantees you'll reach your audience. One can check their mails no matter where they are.

Given below are some advantages of e-mail :

- It has revolutionised the way people work. It helps to respond to customers and colleagues faster.
- Services of this powerful messaging system gives one immediate access to worldwide contacts.
- Delays and inefficiencies in reporting systems can cripple effectiveness. E- mail improves report delivery and distribution both inside and outside the organisation.
- It saves valuable time and is convenient to use.

Let us now look at some of the disadvantages of e-mail :

- Nothing beats face to face communication. It is the best way to build a long lasting relationship.
- E-Mails do not convey the non-verbal cues like a smile or polite tone.
- An ineffective mail can be dangerous leading to loss of productivity and confusion.

However, the advantages outweigh the disadvantages in the case of e-mails.

E-mail Etiquette

Individuals, especially managers, should ensure that they use e-mail in a responsible and business-like manner. Many organisations develop guidelines for effective use of e-mail. These guidelines may helping reducing unnecessary communications and confusion by defining appropriate e-mail content and use.

Because your e-mails reflect both your personality and your professionalism, always be conscious of how your messages will affect the audiences. Some of the key guidelines are discussed below :

1. **Write a meaningful subject line:** Recipients scan the subject line in order to decide whether to open, forward, file or trash a message. Remember your message is not the only one in your recipient's mailbox.
2. **Keep the message focused and readable:** Often recipients only read halfway through a long message, hit 'reply button' as soon as they have something to contribute, and forget to keep reading. This is human nature. So, if your e-mail contains multiple messages that are only loosely related, in order to avoid the risk that your reader will only reply to the first item that grabs his or her attention, you could number your points to ensure that they are all read. If the points are substantial, split them up into separate messages so that the reader can respond, delete, file or forward each item individually. This way you can keep your message focused.

   You may keep in mind the following :
   - Keep your message readable.
   - Use standard capitalisation and spelling.
   - Avoid fancy typefaces.
   - Don't type all in capital letters: It may make the reader feel that you are being aggressive and shouting on him or her.
3. **Avoid attachments:** Put your information in the body of your e-mail whenever possible. Attachments are increasingly dangerous carriers of viruses that take time to download and take up needless space on your recipients' computer.
4. **Identify yourself clearly:** When contacting someone professionally, always include your name, occupation, and any other important identification information in the first few sentences.
5. **Be kind, don't flame:** To 'flame' someone is to write an abusive personal attack. If you find yourself writing in anger, take a break. Take some time to cool off before you hit 'send' button. Don't flame without weighing the consequences.
   - If you flame your boss, that message will probably surface someday when you are up for promotion or you want a letter of recommendation.

- If you flame your colleague or subordinate, then you damage that person's trust in your leadership, and probably you won't get that person's best work in the future.

Praise in public, criticise in private. If you want to complain about someone, do it in person or by telephone, so there won't be any permanent record.

6. **Proofread your message:** Take time to make your message look professional. Revise and edit it carefully before you hit the send button.
7. **Don't assume privacy:** E-mail is not secure. A curious hacker, a criminal or anybody with mean motives can easily intercept your e-mail. In some companies, the e-mail administrator has the ability and authority to read any and all e-mail messages and may fire you, if you write anything inappropriate.
8. **Distinguish between formal and informal situations:** When you are writing to a friend or a close colleague, it is ok to use 'smiley' , abbreviations (LOL – laugh out loud, etc.) and non-standard punctuation and spelling, like the one found in instant messaging and chat rooms. These linguistic shortcuts are generally signs of friendly intimacy. But things are different when you are dealing with a professional or visiting dignitary, because then you would give the impression that you did not really care about the message. Don't use informal language when your reader expects a more formal approach.
9. **Respond promptly:** If you want to appear professional and courteous, make yourself available to your online correspondents.
10. **Show respect and restraint:** While most people know that e-mail is not private, it is good etiquette to ask the sender before forwarding a personal message. Remember that by sending an e-mail message, you are taking up other people's time. And be sure not to send jokes, chain letters, and derogatory comments.
11. **Use the priority feature with care:** Many e-mail packages allow you to assign a priority to your message, such as high, low or normal. Such priority simply helps readers decide how quickly to read and respond to messages. However, if every message you send is 'high priority', readers will begin to disregard the label and question the importance of all your messages. So make sure the priority assigned to your message matches its urgency.

12. **Write short e-mail messages:** Keep your messages short whenever possible. Short, direct messages have a much better chance of being understood and acted upon than long ones. However do not edit them so much that they become incomprehensible to the readers. Make sure to include all the relevant information.

SOME OTHER TECHNOLOGY-BASED COMMUNICATION TOOLS

- **Telephones:** The telephone lets you contact those who may be difficult to reach in person. It can even help you get through to busy people who are nearby. A telephone conversation does lack the visual elements and non-verbal language which often reveals how the message is getting across. However, the vocal cues – tone, pitch, volume, speed, pause and interruptions – can give a fair idea about the other person's reaction to the message.
- **Voice mails:** Voice mail is a high technology version of the answering machine. It allows you to leave the message at any time of the day or night. You will be sure that the recipient will receive the message and that too in your own voice, without any distortions or omissions.
- **Speech recognition softwares:** Many companies are using speech recognition software to provide callers with better customer service. It involves programs that recognise large number of words and natural language patterns. Businesses are using these programs to liberate calling customers from the painful and tedious 'press one, press two' phone menus of voice mail.
- **Mobiles/Cellular phones:** Mobile phones have become an integral and indispensable part of people's lives now. The biggest advantage being that it is easy to contact any person anywhere. A mobile phone gives you more time to communicate. An important conversation can take place anywhere, which puts few restrictions on time, thereby providing better response times to customer or associate enquiries.

  Organisations are using mobile phones to market business nowadays. They use the short messaging service, popularly known as SMS, to effectively advertise their business.
- **Facsimile machines (faxes):** A facsimile machine scans a printed page, converts it into a signal, and transmits the signal over a

telephone line to a receiving fax machine. One can use faxes to send messages across time zones or international boundaries, when a written record is significant or when speed is important.

- **Computers – Desktops/Laptops:** Organisations cannot do away with computers in the modern world. A desktop is the most common type of computer, one that is set up to operate in offices. A laptop computer is portable. Laptops are more expensive than desktops, but if one travels much and needs computing round the clock, it is worth it.
- **PDA – Personal Digital Assistants:** In recent years, more business people and professionals are communicating on the fly, using pocket-sized, hand held devices – known as PDA'S or handheld computers. They store and organise data and contact information. In a very small package, you can have your entire contact list, a calendar and a 'things to do' list.
- **Voice/Audio conferencing:** Audio conference uses conference calls to bring together clients or colleagues at a moments notice, or uses audio streaming to simultaneously reach thousands of individuals across the globe. An audio conference is just a local or national call away with a telephone network, regardless of where you and your participants are. In voice conferencing, five or six people in different locations can hold a conference call using conventional telephone equipment. Voice conferencing saves time.
- **Video conferencing:** When you want to see people you are talking to in a conference call to gauge their reactions and have a clue regarding their non-verbal language, video conferencing fits in aptly. Today, video conferencing can be achieved by adding software and relatively inexpensive hardware to standard desktop computers. It is an excellent example of synchronous conferencing system that takes place between individuals or groups who are usually separated geographically.

IMPACT OF TECHNOLOGY ON COMMUNICATION

Positive Impacts

1. Distance is no longer considered a barrier. An individual can reach people within seconds, thereby revolutionising the concept of communication.

2. *Time saving*: Communication technologies avoid errors and duplication resulting in saving of time. They are speedy and accurate and can transmit quickly, thereby resulting in quicker decision-making. A large quantity of information can be fed into the machines which, in turn, transmit with considerable speed.
3. More people in an organisation have access to more information.
4. The organisational structure has become more streamlined as managers now have increased direct contact with their subordinates.
5. *Labour saving*: New communication technologies are labour saving devices. The 'saved' labour can be utilised for some alternative work.
6. *Reduction of monotony*: Routine repetitive work may lead to dullness or monotony. Mechanisation of communication reduces fatigue of the employees, resulting in improved the efficiency and quality of work.
7. *Standardisation*: It can be achieved through these new technologies which ensure consistency, uniformity in the quality and quantity of work. Office records become uniform and appear more professional, thereby promoting goodwill outside.
8. *Accuracy*: Correctness of message transmission is necessary to enable the receiver to understand in the same spirit and to act accordingly. Systematic and automatic technologies promote accuracy.

Negative Impacts

1. **Cost:** The cost factor cannot be ignored in communication technologies. It includes both the installation cost and the recurring maintenance cost. Some small organisations may find it difficult to afford such costs.
2. **Information overload:** The new communication technologies are accompanied by an increase in information, which leads to psychological, physical and social problems. Other side effects would be anxiety, delayed decision-making, retention problem and reduced attention span.
3. **Do not work without human intelligence:** The technologies are just artificial intelligence, and need human brains to govern and supervise them.
4. **Unemployment:** Mechanisation may cause unemployment.

POINTS TO REMEMBER

- In this 'age of communication', information and wide access to it is considered wealth. Appropriately used, technology can assist individuals and organisations with the work related to writing as well as the creative, thinking aspects.
- The internet is the world's largest computer network. Electronic mail (e-mail) enables users to create, send and read written messages entirely on computer. Because your e-mails reflect both your personality and your professionalism, always ensure how your messages will affect the audiences.
- Other technology based communication tools are telephones, voice mails, speech recognition software, mobile/cellular phones, facsimile machine, PDA's, audio/voice conferencing, and video conferencing.
- Technology in communication has certain positive and negative impacts.

Chapter

10

Writing Effective Business Messages

Learning Objectives

- To understand the steps in writing effective business messages
- To understand the various types of business messages
- To understand the two types of approaches used in business messages
- To learn, briefly, about letters and memos
- To learn, briefly, about reports and proposals

It is insight into human nature that is the key to the communicator's skill. For, whereas the writer is concerned with what he puts into his writing, the communicator is concerned with what the reader gets out of it.

—William Bernbach

INTRODUCTION

Whether an individual is preparing a written or an oral business message, for it to be effective, one needs to plan, organise, draft, revise, edit and proofread. Business messages are so much a part of everyday business that one cannot think of a business without related business messages.

Organisations rely on written communication for many reasons. It provides a permanent record, a necessity in these times. Written documents are also convenient because they can be composed and read when the schedules of both communicators permit, and can be reviewed if necessary.

Written messages have disadvantages too. They require careful preparation and sensitivity to audience

Well-written business documents create a favourable – professional and strong – image. Choosing the right tone and words wins the job interview, lands a new client, cracks a deal and gets a new product approved.

Even with the most advanced office technology, the need for careful preparation of either written or oral messages demands effort.

STEPS IN WRITING EFFECTIVE MESSAGES

For writing effective business messages, keep in mind the following steps :

1. Identify the purpose

- Determine whether the general purpose of your message is to inform, to persuade or collaborate.
- To determine a specific purpose, think of how the audience's ideas or behaviour should be affected by the message.
- Make sure the purpose is worthwhile and realistic.
- Make sure that the time is right for your purpose and the right person is delivering your message.
- Make sure your purpose is acceptable to your organisation.

2. Analyse the audience

- **Identify the primary audience:** If you can reach the decision makers in your audience, other audience members will fall into place. However, in some cases, personnel of relatively low status also influence others in their decisions. The idea is to identify the key audience for whom the business message is targeted.
- **Determine the audience size:** A report for wide distribution style requires a more formal approach, style and format, as compared to the one directed to three or four people in the

organisation. Also, be sure to respond to the needs of individuals. For example, a marketing manager will need different facts as compared to a finance manager.

- **Determine audience composition:** Look for common denominators that tie audience members across differences in culture, education, status or attitude. Include evidence and relevant facts that touch on everybody's area of interest.
- **Gauge the audience's level of understanding:** If audience members share your general background, they will understand your content without difficulty. If not, you must educate them. Include only enough information to achieve your objective. Everything else is irrelevant and must be eliminated; otherwise it will overwhelm the audience, and will divert attention from the key points.
- **Estimate the audience's probable reaction to your message:** There are two approaches to choose from: direct (deductive) approach and indirect (inductive) approach.
  [**Note:** These approaches are explained in detail on page 113]

3. Satisfy audience's needs

- Use the 'you attitude' – that is, speak and write in terms of your audience's wishes, interests, hopes and preferences. When you talk about the other person, you are talking about the thing that most interests him or her.
- Find out what your audience wants to know.
- Provide all the required information and make sure it is accurate, ethical and pertinent.
- Select the right medium for your message by considering factors such as urgency, formality, complexity, confidentiality, emotional content, cost, audience expectation and your need for a permanent record.
- Emphasise the positive aspects of your message.
- Show respect for your audience by using a polite tone.
- Show sensitivity and fairness by using bias-free language, which involves gender bias, racial and ethnic bias, age bias and disability bias.
- Project your company's image in such a way so as to make sure your audience understands that you are speaking for your organisation.

4. Choose your ideas

The ideas you include depend on the type of message you are sending, the situation and the cultural context. Before preparing your business messages, be aware of the two important approaches, namely, direct and indirect approach.

Use the **direct (deductive) approach** when the audience is receptive or will have a favourable or neutral reaction to your message. You begin with the main idea or the best news, followed by all the necessary explanatory details and end with an appropriate, friendly closing. Use this approach in good news and routine messages.

Use the **indirect (inductive) approach** if you think that the audience might react negatively, will be displeased about or resist your message. In this case, do not present the main idea in the first paragraph. Start with a buffer – a relevant, pleasant, and neutral or receiver benefit statement; give an explanation and then introduce the main idea. Use this approach in bad news and persuasive messages.

To choose between the two alternatives, you must analyse your audience's likely reaction to your purpose and message. Audience reaction will probably fall somewhere between the two extremes – an eagerness unwillingness to accept your message. The direct approach is generally fine when audience members are receptive – if they are eager, pleased, interested or even, neutral. And the indirect approach is suited best when the audience is likely to be hostile, displeased, uninterested or unwilling.

However, each message is unique. For example, if you are sending bad news message to outsiders, an indirect approach may be best. On the other hand, if you are drafting a memo to an associate, you may want to get directly to the point, even if the message is unpleasant. The direct approach may be a good choice for long messages, because delaying the main idea can cause confusion and frustration.

To summarise, the choice of a direct and indirect approach depends upon the following factors:

- **Audience reaction:** positive, negative, neutral
- **Message length:** short (letters and memos), or long (reports, proposals and presentations)
- **Message type:** (i) routine, good news and goodwill messages, (ii) bad news messages, (iii) persuasive messages

5. Revising the message

- Message should be readable – use a variety of both long and short sentences, keep paragraphs short, use bullets for emphasis and clarity in headings and sub-headings.

- ❑ Delete unnecessary words and phrases.
- ❑ Use technology to revise the message – spell checkers, grammar checkers and computerised thesauruses can all help with the revision process – but they cannot take the place of good writing and editing skills.
- ❑ The types of details to look for when proofreading include language errors, missing material, design errors, and typographical errors.
- ❑ Vary the style to create a tone that suits the occasion.
- ❑ Use a conversational tone – avoid obsolete and pompous language, intimacy, preaching and bragging, and also humour.
- ❑ Use plain English.
- ❑ Avoid clichés and jargons.

BUSINESS MESSAGES

Written messages take many forms. Although many types of written communication are specialised, the most common are letters and memos, reports and proposals.

Letters and Memos

Most letters and memos are relatively brief documents, generally one or two pages.

Memos are used for routine, day to day exchange of information within an organisation. They use 'To', 'From', 'Date' and 'Subject' headings to emphasise the needs of readers who usually have time only to skim messages. Good memos discuss only one topic and their tone is conversational.

Letters generally go to outsiders, and perform an important public relations function, apart from conveying a message. When you write a letter, you create an image of your company and yourself in the reader's mind. In business deals, precision of writing and clarity of meaning are extremely important. A good letter should be effortless reading that makes the reader want to read more.

Both letters and memos can be classified by function in three categories :

- ❑ Routine, good news and goodwill messages
- ❑ Bad news messages
- ❑ Persuasive messages

Reports and Proposals

Reports and proposals are factual, objective documents that may be distributed to insiders or outsiders, depending on their purpose and subject. They come in many formats – preprinted forms, letters, memos, manuscripts. In length, they range from few to several hundred pages, and are generally more formal in tone as compared to a typical business letter or memo.

(Note: The above mentioned types of business messages are discussed in detail in the coming chapters.)

POINTS TO REMEMBER

- Business messages are so much a part of everyday business that one cannot think of a business without related business messages.
- Whether an individual is preparing a written or an oral business message, to be effective one need to plan, organise, draft, revise, edit and proofread.
- The steps involved in writing effective business messages are – identify the purpose, analyse the audience, satisfy audience's needs, choose the appropriate approach, and revise the message.
- Developing an audience profile and meeting their needs is of utmost importance while preparing for effective business messages.
- Business messages are drafted keeping in mind two important approaches – direct approach and indirect approach.
- Written messages take many forms – letters, memos, reports and proposals.

Chapter

11

Types of Business Messages

Learning Objectives

- To understand the concept of routine, goodwill and good news messages
- To learn the strategy for writing positive messages
- To understand the concept of bad news messages
- To learn the strategy for writing negative messages
- To understand the concept of persuasive messages
- To learn the strategy for writing persuasive messages
- To learn the AIDA plan for persuasive messages
- Learning to draft sales letters

To effectively communicate, we must realise that we are all different in the way we perceive the world and use this understanding as a guide to our communication with others.

—Anthony Robbins

ROUTINE, GOOD NEWS AND GOODWILL MESSAGES

The most straightforward business messages are routine, good news and goodwill messages. If you are announcing a price cut, granting an adjustment, accepting an invitation, or congratulating a colleague, your audience will most likely be pleased to hear from you. If you are providing routine information as part of your regular business, the reaction of your audience will be neutral, neither pleased nor displeased.

A message that will receive a favourable or neutral reaction from your reader is usually easy to write because such a message tells your reader something pleasant or offers useful information.

Some example of good news messages are as given below :

- Answering enquiries
- Granting requests for adjustments
- Approving credit
- Acknowledging orders
- Granting favours
- Job acceptance letters

Goodwill messages may be of the following kinds :

- Appreciation letters
- Congratulatory letters
- Condolence letters

Neutral messages can be announcements about sales and events, procedures, policies and responsibilities, honours, and activities of people.

These messages are organised by the direct approach which has three parts :

1. **Opening:** Best news or the main idea
2. **Middle:** Explanation with all the necessary details and information.
3. **Closing:** Positive, friendly ending, with a willingness to help further.

BAD NEWS MESSAGES

If you are turning down a job applicant, refusing credit, or denying a request for an adjustment, your audience will be disappointed and react negatively. Successful business people know that every person they encounter could be a potential customer, supplier or contributor, which restrains them from blurting out the unpleasant message just like that.

Composing a statement that creates and maintains goodwill towards you and your organisation, and at the same time, conveys bad news will require a great deal of effort.

Some examples of bad news messages are given below :

- Answering non-sales related enquiries, when the information is undesirable
- Refusing adjustments on claims and complaints
- Informing the customer that he/she is at fault regarding a product
- Informing the customer that he/she is mistaken about a service or an account
- Refusing credit
- Declining orders that you cannot fill now or at all
- Declining invitations and requests for favours
- Announcing bad news about prices and services
- Penalising for non-conformity to rules or procedures
- Conveying other bad news like an error in billing, resignation letters, etc.

In negative messages, it is imperative that your tone is appropriate. Keep in mind the consideration and courtesy of the seven C's of communication discussed earlier. The following points must be kept in mind while writing bad news messages :

- Put yourself in the reader's place. The goal is to convince the reader that your decision, although not in his/her favour of reader, is fair and reasonable.
- Avoid using company rules and policies, with no further explanations; in statements like 'It is against company policy to do as you have asked...' include customer benefits or reasons that are behind your company rules and policies.
- Assume that the customer wants to do the right thing, even though he or she may be mistaken.
- Be courteous and shield the reader's pride.
- Talk with, not down to, the reader.

Every bad news message has an objective – to present the unpleasant facts in such a way that the reader will consider you fair and reasonable. These messages are organised by the **indirect approach**. It has the following parts :

1. **Buffer:** Begin your message with reader interest information. The buffer should be pleasant, relevant, honest and neutral in

tone. Avoid misleading the reader into thinking that the news is good.

2. **Explanation and analysis of circumstances:** Include honest, convincing reasons as to why the matter is not being handled in the reader's favour. Explain courteously all relevant facts behind your decision. Mention first the favourable factors, then the unfavourable ones.
3. **Try to convince the reader** that you are acting in their best interests in the long run or according to a company policy that is enforced equally for all.
4. **The decision:** Express your decision clearly near the end of the explanation. The best place for a negative decision is in the middle of a paragraph, and never in a paragraph by itself. Avoid 'refuse', 'cannot grant' and similar negatives.
5. **Closing:** End on a friendly, positive note. Offer assurances that you appreciate the reader as a customer. Express continued interest, service and reader benefit, or sincere wishes for the reader's success. Do not repeat the bad news again.

Sometimes 'bad news messages also take the direct approach'. It depends upon the context and on the particular circumstances like.

- ❑ A routine matter on which the reader is not likely to be disappointed or emotionally involved
- ❑ A reader who is known to prefer reading the bad news in the first paragraph
- ❑ An urgent message that should be called to the reader's attention forcefully.

PERSUASIVE MESSAGES

Many times you want your readers to do something: you wish them to act, to accept a point of view, to follow your wishes, to respond, to change, or not to change. Persuasion has one core purpose: get your reader to support, believe, and act in your favour.

Unlike routine positive messages, they aim to influence audiences who are inclined to resist. Therefore, they are generally longer, more detailed and often depend heavily on strategic planning. While writing a persuasive message, keep in mind the following :

- ❑ Persuasive requests encounter two problems – audiences are busy; and audiences receive many competing requests.
- ❑ Analyse your audience and appeal to their specific needs.

- Establish your credibility which will convince people that you know what you are talking about and that you are not trying to mislead them. Your credibility is your capability of being believed because you are reliable and worthy of confidence. Gain credibility by supporting your arguments with facts such as testimonials, documents, guarantees, and statistics and research results. Your credibility is improved if you name your sources and have good intentions.
- Strive for high ethical standards. To maintain the highest ethics, try to persuade without manipulating.

Use the **indirect approach** when your audience will react unfavourably to your message.

Use the **direct approach** when your message is long or complex, or when the reader prefers directness.

The AIDA Plan

Whether you use a direct or indirect approach, you must convince your reader that your request or idea is reasonable. You have to capture people's attention before you can persuade them to do something. You have to get your audience to consider with an open mind what you have to say. So you have to make an interesting point and provide supporting facts that encourage the audience to continue paying attention.

Organise persuasive messages using the AIDA plan.

- **Attention:** Begin every message with an attention getting statement that is personalised, complete with 'you-attitude', straightforward, relevant, or something that is of real interest or value.
- **Interest:** Build the reader's interest by further explaining the benefits and appealing to the audience's emotions or logic. Both emotional and logical appeals are needed to write successful persuasive messages.

  Emotional appeal: It calls on human feelings, basing the argument on audience needs and sympathies. Use words like success, prestige, comfort, savings, free, value, etc. which put the audience in a certain frame of mind and help them accept your message. But the point to note here is that emotional appeals are not sufficient by themselves; emotions work with logic.

  Logical appeal: It calls on human reason. In order to persuade an audience, a claim is made and then reasons and evidence are given to support it.

- **Desire:** Build desire by showing how your offer can really help the reader.
- **Action:** Suggest a specific step that the audience can take and restate how the audience will benefit by your idea. Provide a convenient means for the reader to take the next step.

Some examples of persuasive messages are given below :

- Requests that require time or personal contributions
- Requests about products and services
- Requests for claims
- Requests for adjustments
- Requesting credit
- Requests for changes in policy
- Request from employer to a reference
- Persuasive sales letters – solicited and unsolicited

SALES LETTERS

The purpose of writing a sales message is to sell the product. It attempts to persuade readers to spend their time and money on the value being offered. It uses the AIDA plan to deliver the message.

Attention

- Design a positive opening that awakens a favourable association with the product.
- Write the opening so that it is appropriate, fresh, honest, interesting, specific and relevant. The techniques used in opening statements can be a comparison or a story, event in reader's life, rhetorical question, enclosed gift, surprise question, a problem the reader may face, quotation or a challenge statement. Remember that clichés are a turn off, avoid them.
- Promise a benefit to the reader.
- Keep the first paragraph short, preferably two to five lines.

Interest

- State information clearly and persuasively, relating to the reader's concerns.
- Develop the central selling point – the single point around which you build your sales message. To determine your product's central selling point, ask – What does the competition offer? What is special about my product? What are buyers really looking for?
- Feature the product in two ways: physical description and reader benefits.
- Describe details of the product: size, shape, colour, scent, texture, sound, etc.

Desire

- Use appeals to support the selling point.
- If the product is valued mainly because of its physical appearance, describe its physical details.
- Provide test results from recognised experts, laboratories or authoritative agencies.
- Anticipate and answer the reader's questions.
- Provide names, with permission only, of satisfied buyers and users.
- Offer a free trial or a guarantee, and refer to samples, if included.

Action

- Clearly state the action you desire.
- Provide specific details on how to order the product or reach your organisation.
- Ease action with reply cards, pre-addressed envelopes, phone numbers and follow up phone calls.
- Offer a special inducement to act now: time limit or situation urgency, special price for a limited time, premium for acting before a certain date, free trial, gift for purchasing the product, no obligation to buy with more information or demonstration, easy payments with no down payment, credit card payments, etc.

A Summary of Different Kinds of Messages

Message Type	*Audience Reaction*	*Approach*	*Opening*	*Body*	*Closing*
Routine, good news goodwill	Pleased or neural	Direct	Begin with the main idea, the request, or the good news	Provide necessary details	Close with a cordial comment
Bad news	Displeased	Indirect	Begin with a neutral statement that acts as a transition to the reasons for the bad news	Give reasons to justify a negative answer. State the bad news, and make a positive suggestion	Close cordially
Persuasive	Uninte-rested	Indirect	Begin with a statement or question that captures attention	Arouse the audience's interest in the subject. Build the audience desire	Request action

POINTS TO REMEMBER

- The most straightforward business messages are routine, good news and goodwill message because your audience will be most likely to be pleased to hear from you.
- Routine, goodwill, and good news messages are organised by the direct approach.
- It is most difficult to write bad news messages as one has to keep in mind the audience reaction, which is hostile, and at the same time maintain goodwill.
- In negative messages, it is imperative that your tone is appropriate.
- Every bad news has an objective – to present the unpleasant facts in such a way that the reader will consider you fair and reasonable. These messages are organised by the indirect approach.
- Persuasion has one core purpose: get your reader to support, believe, and act in your favour.
- Whether you use a direct or indirect approach in a persuasive message, you must convince your reader that your request or idea is reasonable. You have to capture people's attention before you can persuade them to do something.
- Persuasive messages use the AIDA plan – attention, interest, desire and action.
- The purpose in writing a sales message is to sell the product. It attempts to persuade readers to spend their time and money on the value being offered. It uses the AIDA plan to deliver the message.

Chapter

12

Business Reports

Learning Objectives

- To know the five classifications of business reports
- To understand the four types of informational reports
- To learn about the two types of analytical reports
- To understand the steps in writing an effective business report
- To learn about letter reports and standard/optional parts of a letter
- To learn the three letter styles
- To learn how to memo reports
- To learn about long reports – formal reports – and understand its components
- To know what it takes to write an effective report

Never mistake legibility for communication.

—David Carson

A business report is any factual, objective document that serves the business purpose. In other words, a report is a logical presentation of facts and information. Business reports help companies take decisions and solve business problems.

TYPES OF REPORTS

Business reports may be classified in several ways :

- **Voluntary or Authorised reports:** Voluntary reports are prepared at your own initiative. They usually require more detail and support; and more background information on the subject is given. Authorised reports, on the other hand, are prepared at the request of someone else. They require less detail and are organised to the reader's needs.
- **Routine or Special reports:** Routine or periodic reports, like sales or financial reports, are submitted on a recurring basis (daily, weekly, monthly, quarterly, annually). They are commonly prepared on preprinted or computerised forms that are organised in a standard way. Special reports are non-recurring reports that typically present the results of specific, one time studies or investigations, thereby requiring more introduction and background information.
- **Internal or External reports:** Internal reports are designed for use within the organisation. They are less formal and are usually under ten pages (in a memo format). External reports are sent to people outside the organisation. They are formal in nature, and can be either in a letter format (up to five pages) or in a manuscript form (exceeding five pages).
- **Short or Long reports:** Short reports (one to nine pages) discuss just one part of the problem and may not require formal research. On the other hand, long reports (ten pages or more) examine a problem in great detail and generally require extensive research and preparation time. Short and long reports will be taken up in detail later in the chapter.
- **Informational or Analytical reports:** Informational reports focus on facts and the purpose is mainly to explain something or educate readers. In contrast, Analytical reports are designed to solve a problem by convincing readers that the conclusions and recommendations reached are valid and justified based on the data, analysis, and interpretations presented. Information in analytical reports plays a supporting role.

Remember that a single report may have several classifications. For example, a monthly sales report is generally an authorised, routine, internal, short, informational report, whereas a market analysis is an authorised, special, internal, long and analytical report.

Given below are different kinds of informational and analytical reports :

Informational Reports

1. **Reports for monitoring and controlling operations:** These reports help managers find out what is happening in the operations under their control. They expose any problems that exist. They require special attention to accuracy, thoroughness and honesty of content.
2. **Reports for implementing policies and procedures:** Because managers are unable to talk first hand to everyone under them in the organisation, these reports help them to communicate the company's standards.
3. **Reports for complying with government regulations:** These reports explain what a company is doing to conform to government regulations. Government agencies issues instructions on how to write the necessary reports. They are generally prepared on an annual basis and should be honest, thorough and accurate.
4. **Reports for documenting progress:** These reports vary in importance and complexity. It is important to anticipate your reader's needs and to provide the required information clearly and tactfully. Projects or jobs that take place over time must provide regular updates in the form of progress reports, thereby ensuring that they are submitted on a regular basis.

Analytical Reports

1. **Problem-solving reports:** When solving problems, managers need both basic information and detailed analysis to evaluate the possible solutions. These reports provide the management with background information and analysis of options. They typically require secondary or primary research on issues like product demand, growth projections, competitor profiles, company strengths and weaknesses, and sales trends and forecasts.
2. **Proposals:** It is a special type of analytical report designed to get products, plans or projects accepted by others. (Discussed in detail in the next chapter.)

STEPS IN WRITING A BUSINESS REPORT

- **Analyse the situation:** Develop a statement of purpose that defines why you are preparing the report. Select an appropriate report type and develop its preliminary outline.
- **Gather the information:** Access primary and secondary information and process it.
- **Adapt your business report to the audience:** Establish a good relationship with your audience using the 'you-attitude'. Emphasise the positives by establishing your credibility, being polite, using bias free language and projecting the company's image. Select the appropriate channel and medium for your report, whether written, oral or electronic.
- **Decide on format and length:** For brief external reports, choose the letter format. For brief internal reports, choose the memo format. Choose a report length that matches your subject, purpose and audience's expectations.
- **Select an organisational approach:** Use direct approach for audiences that are likely to be receptive to informational and analytical reports. Use indirect approach for audiences that you feel will be skeptical or hostile analytical reports.
- **Choose proper degree of formality:** For informal reports, adopt a personal style, using the pronouns I and you. But certain audiences and situations require a more formal style. Being formal means putting your readers at a distance and establishing a objective, businesslike relationship.
- **Help readers find their way:** Provide headings to improve readability, clarify framework, and indicate shifts in discussion.

SHORT REPORTS

Short reports can be classified into letter reports and memorandum reports (also known as memos).

Letter Reports

All business letters or letter reports have seven standard elements, in the following order :

1. **Heading:** A heading shows where the letter has come from. A letterhead (usually in the top centre) shows the organisation's name, full address and telephone numbers. If not using a letterhead, the heading includes a return address (but no name).

2. **Date:** If you are using a letterhead, place the date at least two blank lines beneath the lowest part of the letterhead. Without letterhead, place the date immediately below the return address.
3. **Inside address:** The inside address depicts the recipient of the letter. Always at the left hand margin, the inside address includes the name and address of the individual, group, or organisation to whom you are writing.

   Begin the inside address one or more lines below the date. Precede the addressee's name with a courtesy title such as Mr, Mrs, Ms, Dr. When in doubt about a women's preference, use Ms plus her name and surname. Current trends suggest Ms as the courtesy title for all business and professional women regardless of their marital status unless they have a professional title. If you do not know whether the person is a man or woman, do not use the courtesy title. Spell out and capitalise titles that precede a person's name, such as Professor or General. The person's organisational title, like Director, may be included in the same line (if it is short) or on the line below; the name of the department may follow.

   For example,

   Mr Amit Dua, Dean

   or

   Ms Shikha Mahajan
   Assistant Vice President

   If the name of the person is unavailable, the letter can be addressed to the department or to a specific position within a department.
4. **Salutation:** Salutations are typed on the second line below the inside address, two lines above the body, and at the left hand margin. When the first line of the inside address is a person's name, the salutation is Dear, Mr or Ms [name]. Base the formality of the salutation on your relationship with the recipient. But remember, whether they are formal or informal, the names are spelled out correctly. Wrong spelling leaves a very bad impression on the recipient and is a glaring evidence of carelessness.
5. **Body:** The body of the letter is your message. Almost all letters are typed single spaced, with two spaces between the paragraphs, before and after the salutation, and before the complimentary close. The body may include indented lists, entire paragraphs indented for emphasis, and even sub-headings.

6. **Complimentary close:** It begins on the second line below the body of the letter. It completely reflects the relationship between you and the person you are writing to. The standard, often used complimentary close are: Sincerely, Sincerely yours, Yours very truly, Cordially. Sometimes people also add Warm regards, Best regards, and Best wishes.
7. **Signature block:** You can include, in the signature area, several identifications like name of your company, your signature, your typewritten name, and your business title. Leave three blank lines for a written signature below the complimentary close, and then include the typed sender's name. Your signature is pen-written above your typed name.

   For example:

   Sincerely yours,

   Savita

   Savita Gupta

   Marketing Manager

Besides these seven standard elements, letter reports can have the following ten additional/optional parts.

1. **Addressee notation:** Letters that have a restricted readership or that must be handled in a special way should include addressee notations like Personal, Confidential or Please forward. This sort of notation appears a double space above the inside address, in all capital letters.
2. **Attention line:** When you want to direct a letter to a particular person or title or department in an organisation, you can use an attention line. It is useful when
   - the writer does not know an individual's name but wants the message to go to a particular title (sales or marketing manager) or department.
   - the writer knows only the recipient's surname.

   The attention line can be placed on the first line and use the company name as the second line of the inside address. It can also be placed between the inside address and salutation, with a blank line before and after it.
3. **Subject line:** It lets the reader know, at a glance, what the letter is all about. It also helps in filing and future reference. It usually appears below the salutation, at left hand margin. Sometimes it is also placed above the salutation. The subject line may use or omit the word 'subject'.

4. **Second page heading:** If the letter is long and an additional page is required, use a second page heading. Some companies have second page letterhead, with the company name and address in a smaller typeface. In any case, the second page heading bears the name of the person or organisation that appears in the first line of inside address, the page number, and the date of the letter. All the following are acceptable.

   Ms. Sujata Rao
   May 11, 2008
   Page 7

   or

   Ms. Sujata Rao, May 11, 2008, Page 7

   or

   Ms. Sujata Rao -7- May 11, 2008

5. **Company name:** Company's name is usually included in the signature block only when the writer is serving as the company's official spokesperson or when letterhead is not used. If included, put it in all capital letters with a double space below the complimentary close.
6. **Reference initials:** It may happen that one person may write or dictate a letter and another person may produce it; reference initials are used to show who helped prepare the letter. They appear at the left margin, a double space below the last line of the signature block. Some key points to be kept in mind are.

- When the writer's name has been included in the signature block, only the preparer's initials are necessary.
- If only the department appears in the signature block, both sets of initials appear, in one of the following forms :

  RSR/sm
  RSR:sm
  RSR:SM

  The first set of initials is the writer's; the second set is the preparer's.

  - Sometimes the writer and signer of a letter are two different people. In that case, it should bear both their initials as well as those of the typist: JFR/RSR/sm (signer, writer, preparer).
  - When businesspeople type their own letters, reference initials are not included.

7. **Enclosure notation:** An enclosure or attachment notation is included to remind your reader to check for any additional pages of information. They appear at the bottom of a letter, one or two lines below the reference initials.
   For example

   Enclosure

   or

   Enclosures (2)

   or

   Enclosures: Resume

   Photograph
8. **Copy notation:** When you want persons other than the addressee to receive a copy of your letter, the names of these persons should be typed just below the reference initials or enclosure notation, whichever is last. Type 'cc' before the copy notation names, if you are sending them a carbon copy. Type 'c', 'pc', or 'copy', if it is a photocopy. Recipients' addresses may be included after their names.
   When you do not want the addressee to know that the other persons are getting a copy of the letter, type 'bc' (blind copy) or 'bpc' (blind photocopy) and the recipients' names on the copies only.
9. **Mailing notation:** You may place a mailing notation (such as Special Delivery, Certified, or Registered Mail) at the bottom of the letter, after reference initials or enclosure notation, (whichever is last) and before copy notations. Another alternative is to place it below the date and above the inside address. For greater visibility, mailing notations may appear in capital letters.
10. **Postscript:** Letters also bear postscripts – afterthoughts to the letter – to emphasise messages or points already in the letter or personal notes. It is the last thing on any letter and added below everything else typed on the page. It may be typed or handwritten, with or without 'P.S.', 'PS', or 'PS:'.

Business letters are usually arranged in one of the **letter styles** described below :

- **Block format:** Every line and each letter part begins at the left margin. This is a common format because it is quick and easy to prepare.

- **Modified block format:** It is the same as block format, except that the date, complimentary close and signature section start near the centre of the page or end at the right margin. This letter style is often used and looks attractive on the page.
- **Modified block with paragraphs indented:** It is the same as modified block format, with an option of indented paragraphs.

SAMPLE OF BLOCK FORMAT

--------------------.

--.

------------.

(Every line and each letter part begins at the left margin).

SAMPLE OF MODIFIED BLOCK FORMAT

Date---------------

--------------------.

--.

------------.

---Complimentary close---------

--Signature section----------------

(It is the same as block format, except that the date, complimentary close and signature section start at the right margin).

SAMPLE OF MODIFIED BLOCK WITH INDENTED PARAGRAPHS

Date---------------

-----------------.

----------------------------.

------------.

---Complimentary close---------

--Signature section----------------

(It is the same as modified block format, with an option of indented paragraphs. The line of the next paragraph starts where the line of the previous paragraph ends).

Punctuation Styles

Letter reports may use any of the following styles of punctuation.

- **Open style:** No line of any part of the letter (except the body) has any punctuation, unless an abbreviation requires a period (.)
- **Mixed style:** Punctuation is used in this style. A comma follows the salutation and complimentary close.

Memorandum Reports (Memos)

In contrast to the letter, which is directed outside the organisation, the memorandum goes within the organisation. It is the most common form of written communication between people or departments.

Parts of a Memorandum

Standard memos consist of a heading with TO, FROM, DATE, and SUBJECT (with a blank line between). Many organisations have pre printed memo forms, in which the word MESSAGE also appears.

When preparing a memo, include a title such as MEMO or INTEROFFICE CORRESPONDENCE (all in capitals), centered at the top of the page or aligned with left margin, as shown below :

MEMO

TO:
DATE:
FROM:

SUBJECT:

or

MEMO

TO:	DATE:
FROM:	SUBJECT:

You can arrange these four pieces of information in any order.

While writing a memo, remember the following :

1. **Courtesy title:** You do not need to use courtesy titles anywhere in a memo; first initials and last names, first names, or even initials are sufficient. However, it varies with the situation and also organisational practices. A courtesy title such as Mr, Mrs, Ms, before your reader's name may be used, depending upon your relationship with the reader (superior or subordinate), and the level of formality in the organisation. But do remember to omit your title before your own name.
2. **Subject line:** The subject line of a memo helps busy readers quickly find out what your memo is all about. It must make the content of the memo clear.
3. **Body:** Start the body of the memo on the second or third line below the heading. It is not centered on the page and is lined up evenly on the left. Like the body of the letter, it is usually double spaced. If the memo is very short, you may double space it also.
4. **Second page:** If the memo carries over to a second page, head the second page in the same manner as that of a letter report.

5. **Writer's initials:** Unlike a letter, a memo does not require a complimentary close or a signature, because your name is already prominent at the top.
6. **Other elements:** Treat elements such as reference initials, enclosure notations, and copy notations just as you would in a letter.

LONG REPORTS

Long report, also known as formal report, does not mean more formal language; it means the report is more detailed, more complex in structure. The manuscript format and impersonal tone of a formal report convey an impression of professionalism. It can be either short (fewer than ten pages) or long (ten pages or more). It can be informational or analytical. It may be targeted to readers outside or inside an organisation.

The three basic components/divisions of a formal report are as follows :

- Prefatory parts
- Text
- Supplementary parts

Prefatory Parts

Prefatory parts are front end materials that provide key preliminary information so that readers can decide whether, and how, to read the report. Although these parts are placed before the text of the report, they are not written until the text of the report has been written, because they directly reflect the contents. Prefatory parts include the following :

1. **Cover:** Many companies have standard covers for reports, made of heavy paper imprinted with the company's name and logo. Report titles are either printed on these covers or attached with gummed labels. If the organisation has no standard covers, look for a cover that is attractive, convenient and appropriate to the subject-matter.

   Choose a report title that is informative (the who, what, when, where, why and how of the subject), but not too long. Try to be reasonably concise.
2. **Title fly and title page:** The title fly is a plain sheet of paper with only the title of the report on it. It adds a touch of formality, and is optional.

   The title page includes. (i) the title of the report, (ii) the name, title, and address of the person, group, or organisation for which the report is prepared (preceded by words like 'Prepared for' or 'Submitted to') (iii) the name, title, and address of the person, group, or organisation that prepared the report (preceded by words like 'Prepared by' or 'Submitted by'); and (iv) the date on which the report was submitted.

3. **Letter of authorisation:** If a written authority is received to prepare the report, the letter is included in the report. The letter of authorisation is a document requesting that a report be prepared. It typically specifies the problem, scope, time and money restrictions, special instructions, and due date.
4. **Letter of transmittal:** It conveys your report to your audience. In a book, this section is called a preface. The letter of transmittal says what you would say if you were handing the report directly to the reader; that is why the style is less formal than the rest of the report. Conversational language and personal pronouns like I, you and we can be used. It appears right before the table of contents.

   Begin with the main idea, officially conveying the report to the readers and summarising its purpose. The rest includes information about the scope of the report, the methods used to complete the study, and the apparent limitations. If the report does not have a synopsis, the letter of transmittal may summarise the major findings, conclusions and recommendations.
5. **Table of contents:** The table of contents, titled simply 'contents', indicates in outline form the sequence of the information in the report. The headings used in the text of the report are the basis for the table of contents. It is prepared after the other parts of the report have been typed, so that the page numbers for each heading can be inserted. The headings should be worded exactly as they are in the text of the report. Also listed are the prefatory parts and the supplementary parts.
6. **List of illustrations:** Some reports refer to all visual aids as illustrations or exhibits, while in other reports, tables are labeled separately from other types of visual aids, which are called figures. The list of illustrations gives their titles and page numbers. If you have enough space on a single page, include the list of illustrations directly beneath the table of contents. Otherwise, put the list on the page after the contents page.
7. **Synopsis or executive summary:** A synopsis is a brief overview (one page or less) of a report's most important points, designed

to give readers a quick preview of the contents. Because it is a concise representation of the whole report, sometimes it is distributed separately to a wide audience; then interested readers can request a copy of the entire report.

Many business report writers prefer to include an executive summary instead of a synopsis. Whereas a synopsis outlines the main points of the report, an executive summary is a fully developed 'mini version' of the report itself. Executive summaries are more comprehensive than synopsis; may contain headings and even visual aids. Executive summaries are intended for readers who lack the time or motivation to study the complete report. It is often organised in the same way as the report. Executive summary is a popular shortcut, so remember to put enough information in it so that an executive can make a decision without reading the entire report.

Text of the Report

The three main text parts of a report are.

1. **Introduction:** A good introduction invites the audience to continue reading by telling them what the report is all about, why the audience should be concerned, and how the report is organised. If your report has an executive summary, make the introduction relatively brief (due to the repetition of the points).
2. **Body:** This section contains conclusions, recommendations, analysis, logic and the interpretation of the information. Balance the body of the report with adequate data in paragraph format and tables and charts. Too much data in the reports prove to be dull and monotonous for readers and increases the chances of losing them. The extra information can be adjusted in the supplementary parts.
3. **Closing:** The closing of the report should summarise the main idea of the report, highlight the conclusions or recommendations, and list any courses of action you expect the reader to take. In a long report, this section can be labeled as 'Conclusions and Recommendations'.

Supplementary Parts

Supplementary parts follow the text of the report and provide information for readers who seek more detailed information. They are more common in long reports than in short ones.

1. **Appendix:** An appendix contains materials related to the report but not included in the text because they are too lengthy and lack direct relevance. Well-designed appendices provide enough but not too much additional information. It includes sample questionnaires, sample forms, computer printouts, statistical formulae, financial statements and spreadsheets, copies of important documents, and complex illustrations.
   Some organisations specify that all visual aids should be placed in an appendix, but some contend that they should be put in the text body, with the exception of visuals that are too large to fit on one page or are only indirectly relevant to the report, which may be placed in an appendix. All appendices should be mentioned in the text and listed in the table of contents.
2. **Bibliography:** A bibliography is a list of secondary sources consulted when preparing the report. In addition to it, some report writers prefer to cite references in the report text. Acknowledging sources in the body of report demonstrates that you have thoroughly researched the topic. Furthermore, mentioning names of well-known or important authorities on the subject helps build credibility for your message.
3. **Glossary:** When the report includes any terms that have several interpretations, definitions should be inserted, which makes a glossary at the end preferable. Mention in the introduction that the report includes glossary, which will be useful for readers to check some meanings.
4. **Index:** The index lists topics alphabetically, along with the pages on which they occur. Only very long reports have an index.

EFFECTIVE REPORT WRITING

The content and quality of reports influences professional success, because they demonstrate how well you think, gather and analyse data, draw conclusions and develop and support your recommendations. To create successful and effective reports, your content should be :

- **Accurate:** Information presented in the report must be factually correct and error free.
- **Complete:** Include all the information necessary for readers to understand the situation, problem, or proposal, and to facilitate decisions. Support your information with illustrations, explanations and facts. Adopt a 'you-attitude', thereby telling them what they need to know.

- **Balanced:** Be ethical and present all sides of the issue fairly. Include all the essential information. Even in brief reports, include enough information so that the readers can grasp the issue being presented. Omitting relevant information or facts can make the report unjust and biased.
- **Structured clearly and logically:** Make your report readable by making your sentences appear uncluttered, by using well-chosen words and proceeding logically.
- **Documented properly:** If using primary and secondary sources for the report, be sure to properly document it and give credit to the sources, thereby avoiding plagiarism.

POINTS TO REMEMBER

- A business report is any factual, objective document that serves a business purpose. Business reports help companies take decisions and solve business problems.
- Reports can be classified in five ways: voluntary or authorised, routine or special, external or internal, short or long, informational and analytical.
- Informational reports are further classified in four categories – Reports for Monitoring and Controlling Operations; Reports for Implementing Policies and Procedures; Reports for Complying with Government Regulations; Reports for Documenting Progress.
- Analytical reports are further classified as problem-solving reports and proposals.
- Certain guidelines should be kept in mind while formulating effective business reports.
- Short reports can be classified into letter reports and memos.
- All business letters include seven standard elements and some optional/additional elements.
- All memo reports have four major elements – to, from, date and subject.
- Business letters are usually arranged in one of the letter styles – block format, modified block format, modified block format with indented paragraphs.
- Writers have two punctuation styles to choose from – open style and mixed style.
- Long reports or formal report does not mean more formal language; it means the report is more detailed, more complex in structure.

- The three basic divisions of a formal report are as follows - prefatory parts, text, supplementary parts.
- The content and quality of reports influence professional success, because they demonstrate how well you think, gather and analyse data, draw conclusions and develop and support your recommendations.

Chapter

13

Business Proposals

Learning Objectives

- To know the different types of proposals
- To understand the type of approach used for proposals
- To understand the components of a long (formal) proposal
- To understand the components of a short proposal
- To learn the steps in writing effective proposals

Words are, of course, the most powerful drug used by mankind.

—Rudyard Kipling

A proposal is a special type of analytical report designed to get products, plans or projects accepted by others. They include bids to perform work under a contract and pleas for financial support from outsiders. Their acceptance can lead to significant operational improvements, new business, additional jobs and safer working conditions. Proposals can be of one or two pages, or they can be hundreds of pages.

Persuasion lies at the heart of proposal writing. You get your reader to do something, to accept your written plan for completing a task. It does not matter whether the proposal is short or long, what matters is the structure applied to writing good proposals.

TYPES OF PROPOSALS

Internal Proposals and External Proposals

Internal proposals are submitted to decision-makers in one's own organisation. They have two primary purposes (i) to seek approval for a project or course of action (such as revising recruiting procedures, changing the company's training programmes, reorganising a department, engaging in a special study, or adopting a more efficient and effective way of doing something), or (ii) to request additional resources (such as capital assets, human resources or operating funds).

Internal proposals are prepared with extra care because they advocate a change and the audience may feel threatened by the plan.

External proposals are submitted to decision-makers outside the organisation, such as current or potential clients or government agencies. Like internal proposals, they seek approval for projects and funds.

However, there are certain striking differences. Firstly, external proposals are legally binding. Unlike internal proposals, they form the basis of a contract if approval is granted, so they are prepared with extreme care. Secondly, external proposals compete for a client's business. In an internal proposal, the company knows about itself and its operation. There is hardly any need for stating and proving of company's credentials. But, in external proposal, the audience may not know the company, so the proposal must convince readers that the organisation is the best source of a product or service. Therefore, considerable space is devoted to explaining your experience, qualifications, facilities and equipment. Thirdly, because external proposals are directed to outsiders, they are more formal than internal proposals.

Solicited Proposals and Unsolicited Proposals

Solicited proposals are generally prepared at the request of external parties who need something done, but can also be requested by internal sources such as management or the board of directors. Some external parties prepare an invitation to bid on their contract, called a **Request for proposal (RFP)**, which includes instructions that specify the exact type of work to be performed alongwith the guidelines on how and when the company wants the work completed. RFP is responded by preparing a proposal that shows how you would meet the potential customer's needs.

Unsolicited proposals are initiated by organisations attempting to obtain business or funding without a specific invitation from a potential client. They may also be initiated within the organisation, by the employees and managers who wish to convince company insiders to adopt a programme, policy, or idea. In simple words, the writer makes the first move with an unsolicited proposal.

An important difference between solicited and unsolicited proposals is that in the latter, the reader may not know about the problem you are addressing, so the proposal must convince the reader that a problem exists and that you can solve it. Thus, considerable time is devoted to explaining and convincing the reader that there is need to take an action.

Choosing the Approach

- Use a direct approach with solicited proposals. The audience will be more receptive since the problem and the solution have already been identified. The writer submits a proposal for the work specified in RFP, issued by the prospective client, and structures the proposal using the direct approach, focusing on the recommendation.
- Use indirect approach with unsolicited proposals because the reader must be first convinced that a problem exists and credibility also has to be established. To convince the reader that your recommendations are solid and logical, you unfold the solutions to the problem using logical arguments, with the sole goal in mind – to persuade readers to accept your idea and award you a contract.

LONG PROPOSALS

The goal of a proposal is to impress readers with your professionalism and to make your service and your company stand out. This goal is best achieved through a structured and deliberate approach. Long proposals or formal proposals contain many of the same components as other formal reports. However, there are certain differences in the prefatory parts, text of the proposal, and the supplementary parts.

Prefatory Parts

The cover, title fly, title page, table of contents, and list of illustrations are drafted in the same manner as in formal reports (*see* previous chapter). Other prefatory parts are handled differently.

- **Copy of RFP (request for proposal):** Instead of the Letter of authorisation, a formal proposal may have the copy of the RFP, which is a letter or memo soliciting a proposal or a bid for a particular project. If the RFP is too long and detailed, then include only its introductory part.
- **Synopsis or executive summary:** Although a synopsis or an executive summary for the reader's convenience can be included if the proposal is quite long, but these components are often less useful in a formal proposal than they are in a formal report. If the proposal is unsolicited, the letter of transmittal will already convey the information, thereby making the synopsis repetitive and pointless. Even in a solicited proposal, the reader would be already committed to studying the proposal and the introduction would provide the adequate contents. In short, most proposals do not require a synopsis or an executive summary.
- **Letter of transmittal:** The way the letter of transmittal is drafted depends on whether the proposal is solicited or unsolicited. In the solicited proposal, the letter of transmittal follows the pattern for good news messages (direct approach), highlighting the aspects which give competitive advantage. In the unsolicited proposal, the transmittal letter follows the pattern of persuasive messages (AIDA plan). The letter must persuade the reader that there is something worthwhile that justifies the time required to read the entire proposal. All in all, a transmittal letter must be convincing.

Text of the Proposal

Three main text parts of a proposal are:

1. Proposal Introduction

The introduction presents and summarises the problem you want to solve and your solutions. If the proposal is solicited, its introduction should refer to the RFP (Request for Proposal); if unsolicited, its introduction should mention factors that led you to submit the proposal.

You might mention mutual acquaintances, or previous conversations you have had with the readers. The following topics are covered in a proposal introduction :

- **Background or statement of the problem:** Briefly reviews the reader's situation and establishes a need for action. Readers may not perceive problem or opportunity as you do; therefore convincing them becomes necessary in unsolicited proposals. Discuss what is relevant and meaningful to the reader.
- **Solution:** Briefly describe the changes you propose and highlight your key selling features and benefits.
- **Scope:** States the boundaries of the proposal – what you will and will not do.

In short proposals, these elements will be discussed in brief. For long, formal proposals, each of these topics have separate sub-headings and several pages of discussion.

2. Proposal Body

The proposal body has the same purpose as the report body. It gives details on the proposed solution, and provides facts and evidence to support the conclusions. It also includes.

- **Proposed approach:** This section describes what you are offering to the reader: your concept, product or service. To convince readers that your proposal is logical and has merits, adopt a 'you attitude' and focus on the strengths of your offer. In short, demonstrate the superiority of your ideas, products or services.
- **Work plan:** Describe how you will accomplish the task. Explain the steps you will take, their timing, the methods or resources you will use, and the personnel responsible. Include a timeline highlighting critical dates. For solicited proposals, make sure your dates match those in RFP.
- **Statement of qualifications:** In this section, demonstrate that you have the personnel, facilities and experience to do a competent job.
- **Cost:** It can make or break your proposal, because a high price can lose the bid and low price will doom you. Estimating costs is difficult, so prove that your costs are realistic by breaking them down in detail. The more detailed your cost proposal is, the more credibility your estimates will have.

3. Proposal Closing

The final section of the proposal summarises the key points of the proposal, emphasises the benefits that the readers will realise from your solutions, summarises the merits of your approach, re-emphasises why you and your firm are the best ones to do the work, and asks for a decision from the client. This section should be relatively brief, assertive and confident.

Supplementary Parts

With the exception of an occasional appendix, most proposals have few supplementary parts.

SHORT PROPOSALS

Short proposals (less formal in nature) include the following parts :

1. Letter of transmittal
2. Executive summary
3. Body of the proposal with the complete information

STEPS IN WRITING EFFECTIVE PROPOSALS

The general purpose of any proposal is to persuade its readers to do something. Thus, writing for a proposal is similar to writing a persuasive sales message. Your proposal must sell your ideas, products, services, methods and company. The AIDA plan is used to gain attention, build interest, create desire and motivate action. Some additional tips for writing effective proposals are as follows :

- **Demonstrate your knowledge:** Everything you write should show your reader that you have the knowledge and experience to solve the problem.
- **Provide concrete examples:** Readers will demand hard facts in spite of your enthusiasm and good intentions. Avoid vague, unsupported generalisations. Provide quantifiable details as to how much money your proposed solution will save. Spell out the plan and give details on how the job will be done. Such concrete examples persuade readers.
- **Research the competition:** Use trade publications and internet to become familiar with your competitors product lines, services and prices. This approach is effective if you are competing with others.
- **Prove that your proposal is logical and workable:** The proposal must be appropriate and feasible for the audience.

- **Adopt a 'you-attitude':** Relate your product, service, or personnel to the reader's exact needs either as stated in the RFP in the solicited proposals; or as discovered by your investigations in the unsolicited proposals.
- **Package your proposal attractively:** Make sure your proposal is inviting and readable. It should convey an air of professionalism. Any errors, omissions or inconsistencies will be viewed in a bad light and will likely withhold approval.
- **Be realistic as to what you can accomplish:** Avoid over-extending your and your company's capabilities.
- Be precise with the time schedule.
- Be exact to the scope: what you will and will not do.

POINTS TO REMEMBER

- A proposal is a special type of analytical report designed to get products, plans or projects accepted by others.
- Proposals can be classified into – external or internal proposals, solicited or unsolicited proposals.
- Choose the appropriate approach – direct or indirect – to formulate proposals.
- The goal of a proposal is to impress readers with your professionalism and to make your service and your company stand out. This goal is best achieved through a structured and deliberate approach. Formal proposals contain many of the same components as other formal reports.
- Writing for a proposal is similar to writing a persuasive sales message. Your proposal must sell your ideas, products, services, methods and company. AIDA plan is used to gain attention, build interest, create desire and motivate action.

Chapter

14

Resumes and Application Letters

Learning Objectives

- To learn the process of planning and writing an effective resume
- To know the two types of resume and their advantages and disadvantages
- To know the contents of a resume
- To learn the process of revising and proofreading a resume
- Answering some relevant questions regarding drafting a resume
- To learn drafting an application letter
- To know the types of application letters
- Following the AIDA plan for writing an application letter

Self-expression must pass into communication for its fulfillment.

—Pearl S. Buck

While looking for employment, you will need to send out messages such as resumes and application letters. Whenever you send out such employment messages, you have an opportunity to demonstrate your communication skills – skills valued highly by the majority of employers. To distinguish you from all the other people looking for work, you need to start with a well-written resume. In fact, your success in finding a job will depend on how carefully you plan, write and complete your resume.

RESUME

A resume is a persuasive summary of your qualifications for employment. If you are in the job market, having a resume makes you appear well organised and prepared. When you are employed, having an up-to-date resume makes it easier to take advantage of opportunities that may come up for an even better job.

A resume is a structured, written summary of a person's education, employment background, and job qualifications. The fact is that a resume is a form of self-advertising. It is intended to stimulate an employer's interest in you – in meeting you and learning more about you. A successful resume inspires a prospective employer to invite you to an interview.

THE PROCESS OF PREPARING AN EFFECTIVE RESUME

Planning the Resume

- **Analyse your purpose and audience:** The purpose of writing a resume is to build interest – not to tell readers everything about you. Since you have already completed a good deal of research on specific companies, you should know quite a bit about the organisations you are applying to. Try to put yourself in the audience's position so that your resume is tailored to satisfy their needs.
- **Gather relevant information:** Gather every piece of information you can think of, including all the specific dates, duties and accomplishments of any previous jobs you have held. Collect every piece of relevant educational experience that adds to your qualifications, such as formal degrees, skill certificates, academic awards, or scholarships. In short, every bit of information should be at your finger tips before you start composing the resume.
- **Tailor your resume to your audience:** Ask yourself: What key qualifications will this employer be looking for? Which of these qualifications are your strengths? What quality will set you apart from the other candidates? What are your greatest

accomplishments? Then tailor your resume to fit diverse situations and employers. Adopt a 'you-attitude' and think about your résumé from the employer's perspective.

Always remember that a good resume is flexible and can be customised for various situations and employers. Don't exaggerate and alter the past or claim skills you don't have. Don't state your negatives, and focus on the strengths.

Writing the Resume

To write a successful resume, seven qualities need to be conveyed to the seeking employers. You want to show that you

- think in terms of results
- know how to get things done
- are well-rounded
- show signs of progress
- have personal standards of excellence
- are flexible and willing to try new things
- possess strong communication skills.

Organise your resume around your strengths: to focus attention on your strongest points, select an appropriate and relevant organisational pattern, that is, make your resume chronological or functional.

The Chronological Resume

The work experience section dominates in this type of resume and is placed in the most prominent slot, immediately after the name, and address, and the objective. This section includes listing your jobs sequentially in reverse order, beginning with the most recent position and working backward toward earlier jobs. Under each listing, describe your responsibilities and accomplishments, giving the most recent space to recent positions. If you are just graduating from college, you can vary this chronological approach by putting your educational qualifications, thereby focusing attention on your academic credentials. The chronological resume is the most common and the most preferred way to organise a resume. The advantages of this approach are :

- Employers are familiar with it and can easily find information.
- It highlights growth and career progression.
- It is especially appropriate if you have a strong employment history and are aiming for a job that builds on your current career path.

The Functional Resume

A functional resume emphasises a list of skills and accomplishments, thereby focusing attention on your areas of competence. The employment history and academic experience is relegated to subordinate sections. This type of resume is useful for people who are just entering the job market, want to redirect their careers, or have little continuous career related experience. The advantages of functional resume are.

- The employers can easily see what you can do for them
- You can de-emphasise any lack of career progress or lengthy unemployment.

The Contents of a Resume

1. **Name and address:** The first thing an employer wants to know is who you are and where you can be reached – your name, address, phone number, email-id. Many resume headings are nothing more than the name and address centered at the top of the page. Entering the word 'resume' is optional.
2. **Career objective:** The goal of inserting a career objective is to generate interest immediately. Make it effective by being as specific as possible. An alternative is to include a mini summary of your qualifications that highlights your strongest points, particularly if you have varied experience. Some people opt to include this information in the cover letter accompanying the resume. Make sure to make this section strong, concise and convincing.
3. **Education:** If education is your strongest selling point, discuss it thoroughly and highlight it visually. Include school/college names, locations, dates attended, and degrees of certificates attended (insert abbreviations for your degrees). If you did something outstanding there, such information may be added. Decide whether to include grade point average – if it is high, it should be included, if it is low, omit it. If you are working on an uncompleted degree, include in parentheses the date of completion. Showcase your qualifications by listing courses that have directly equipped you for the job you are seeking, and indicate any scholarships, awards or academic honours you have received.

   Education is generally given less emphasis after you have worked for a year or more. If work experience is your strongest qualification, mention education later in the resume and provide less detail.

4. **Work Experience:** This section helps the employers to evaluate whether you have the necessary background for a current position. Tailor your description to highlight the relationship between the previous responsibilities and your target field. Showcase the skills you have developed and your progression of jobs from lesser to higher responsibility.

   When describing your work experience, list your jobs in chronological order. This section lists: name and location of the employer; what the organisation does (if it is not clear from its name); your functional title; how long you worked there; your duties and responsibilities; your significant achievements and contributions.

5. **Activities and achievements:** Your resume should also describe any voluntary activities that demonstrate your abilities. List projects that require teamwork, leadership, cooperation, etc. Additional items often include offices held, athletic or creative accomplishments, published materials, fluency in foreign languages, speaking awards (debate, extempore contests), and fundraising or community service activities.

   Receiving any awards deserves a mention in a resume.

6. **Personal data (optional):** Experts advise to leave off the personal data section. Although no law forbids you from volunteering personal information, you must be careful about including information that could encourage discrimination. Civil rights laws prohibit employers from discriminating on the basis of gender, marital or family status, age, race, religion, national origin, and physical or mental disability.

7. **Miscellaneous facts:** You may also include facts that are relevant to your career objective. You might title a special section 'computer skills' and showcase your computer expertise; or 'language skills' and demonstrate your command of other languages.

8. **References (optional):** Employers nowadays often ask prior to or just after the interview for a list of references. Often the phrase 'references available on request' is the last statement at the end of a resume. However, if you are including references, ensure the following things :

   - Limit your list to three individuals, complete with information about where they may be reached via phone, fax, letter or e-mail.
   - Avoid including relatives as references.

- Choose individuals such as former work supervisors, professors, colleagues or business friends.
- Be sure you have the permission of the individual whose name you are using as a reference.

Revising the Resume

You need to revise your resume, produce it in an appropriate from and proofread it for any errors. The perfect resume responds to the reader's needs and preferences and avoids some common faults like.

- **Too long:** Ideally a resume should be limited to one page. It should be concise, relevant and to the point.
- **Too short:** It should also not be too short, thereby giving not enough information for proper evaluation.
- **Hard to read:** Lack of white space (space free of text work or artwork) and devices such as indentions or boldfacing makes the reader's job difficult.
- **Wordy:** Descriptions should not be verbose. Use of simple and plain English is favoured.
- **Too slick:** The resume should not seem to have been written by someone other than the applicant, which raises questions on his/her credibility.
- **Amateurish:** Awkward presentation of resume shows that the applicant has little understanding of the business world or of a particular industry.
- **Poorly reproduced:** The print is faint and difficult to read.
- **Misspelled and ungrammatical:** Candidates who make spelling and grammatical mistakes lack good verbal skills, which are considered important by the employers those jobs.
- **Boastful:** The resume should not sound boastful.
- **Dishonest:** Try to be truthful and honest while providing the details of expertise, work experience and academic qualifications in your resume.
- **Gimmicky:** Don't structure or decorate the resume in order to grab attention.

The key characteristics of a good resume are – neatness, simplicity, accuracy and honesty. Pay close attention to mechanics and details. Once the resume is complete, update it continuously.

FYI – For Your Information

1. Should I limit my resume to one page?

A one page resume is sufficient, but do fill the page. However, according to experts, the average resume is now two pages. If you use more than one page, the second page should have at least 10 to 12 lines. Staple the second sheet to the first one, so that readers who skim see the staple and know that there's more. Always leave less important information for the second page. Put your name, or page 2 or 'cont...' on the second page.

2. What are the guidelines to be kept in mind while sending the resume in an e- mail message?

- Use a personal e-mail account, not your employer's.
- Avoid silly and unprofessional e-mail addresses. For example, instead of bubbles @ rediffmail.com, use your name @ rediffmail.com.
- Send individual, targeted messages rather than mass mailings.
- Write a simple subject line.

APPLICATION LETTERS

Whenever you submit your resume, accompany it with a cover, or application letter to let readers know what you are sending, why you are sending it, and how they can benefit from reading it. Because your application letter is in your own style (rather than the shorthand style of resume), it gives you a chance to show your communication skills and personality.

Always send your resume and application letter together, because each has a unique job to perform. The purpose of a resume is to get employers interested enough to contact you for an interview. The purpose of an application letter is to get employers interested enough to read your resume.

Try to put yourself in the reader's shoes, and remember that this person's inbox is probably flowing with resumes and cover letters. So respect your reader's time. Steer clear of gimmicks, and keep the application letter straightforward, fact based, short and professional.

Some effective tips for writing an application letter are given below :

- **Be specific:** Avoid general objectives. Be clear about the kind of opportunity and industry you are looking for.

- **Include salary:** If you have been working in your field, include your current salary. But make sure that the readers understand that this is not a demand, but just intended to inform.
- **Make e-mail covers even shorter:** When sending cover letters by e-mail, make them shorter as compared to traditional letters. E-mail readers want the gist quickly.
- **Aim for high quality:** Meticulously check your spelling, mechanics and grammar.

Types of Application Letters

1. **Solicited application letter:** It is written in response to an announced job opening. In this, you usually know what qualifications the organization is seeking. You will also have more competition, as hundreds of applicants will be vying for the same job.
2. **Unsolicited application letter:** It is sent to an organisation that has not announced an opening. This letter stands a better chance of being read and receiving individualised attention.

Both solicited and unsolicited application letters present your qualifications in a similar manner. The main difference is in the opening paragraph. In a solicited letter, you need no special attention-getting devices, because you are invited to apply; whereas in an unsolicited letter, the reader's attention and interest has to be captured.

Writing an Application Letter

Follow the AIDA approach when writing an effective application letter: attention, interest, desire and action.

1. Attention (the opening paragraph)

- Open the letter by capturing the reader's attention in a businesslike way.
- Use a summary, name, source, news, personalised or creative opening.
- State that you are applying for a job, and identify the position or type of work you seek.

2. Interest and Desire (next several paragraphs)

- Present your key qualifications for the job, highlighting what is on your resume: job related education, or relevant work experience.
- Adopt a mature, businesslike tone.
- Eliminate boasting and exaggeration.

- Demonstrate your knowledge of the organisation by citing its trends and operations in the industry.
- Link your education, experience and personal qualities to the job requirements.
- Provide evidence that you can learn quickly, work hard, handle responsibility and get along with others.
- If asked to state salary requirements in your letter, state current or desired salary range.
- Refer the reader to the enclosed resume.

3. Action (the closing paragraph)

- Request an interview at the reader's convenience.
- Make it easy to comply with your request by providing your phone number (with the area code) and stating the best time to reach you.
- Express your appreciation for an opportunity to have an interview.
- Repeat your strongest qualification briefly, to reinforce the claim that you can contribute to the organisation.

EXAMPLE OF CHRONOLOGICAL RESUME

Name: SAKSHI SHARMA
Address: 1728, Greater Kailash, New Delhi – 1100034
Mob: 9999911111
Email: daisysharma@rediffmail.com

CAREER OBJECTIVE

Dedicated administrative professional offers versatile skills and experience supporting key executives. Extensive experience in office and facilities management, meeting planning, and computer applications. Good organiser, who can lead, train and motivate others.

EXPERIENCE

March 1999 to present: Office Administrator, XYZ Pvt. Ltd

- Scheduling and maintaining appointments, files and travel
- Coordinating luncheon meetings
- Coordinating building issues, furniture, office machines
- Ordering office supplies
- Composing correspondence and completing monthly reports

October 1995 to March 1999: Administrative assistant, ABC Pvt. Ltd

- Assisted accountant and various levels of support staff
- Served as liaison between corporate and branch offices
- Supervised clerical staff
- Typed contracts, agreements and proposals
- Maintained files for legal counsel
- Dealt with vendors
- Evaluated monthly performance reviews
- Ordered and proofread business cards

ACHIEVEMENTS

Employee of the month at ABC, Pvt. Ltd in March 1997

Won several prizes at college level for debates, quiz and extempore competitions

EDUCATION

1993 to 1995: Office management and organisational courses, Delhi University, Delhi

1990 to 1993: Bachelor of Business Administration, Delhi University, Delhi

TECHNICAL SKILLS

Attended seminars on time management, communication skills, motivating employees

LANGUAGE PROFICIENCY: Fluent in German and Spanish

COMPUTER SKILLS: windows, word, excel, PowerPoint, outlook e-mail, internet

References available on request.

EXAMPLE OF FUNCTIONAL RESUME

Name: SAKSHI SHARMA
Address: 1728, Greater Kailash, New Delhi – 1100034
Mob: 9999911111
Email: daisysharma@rediffmail.com

CAREER OBJECTIVE

A highly motivated college graduate with a passion for art and history seeks an administration position in which I can complement the existing environment while developing new avenues for growth.

SKILLS

Fluent in English, Spanish, German and French

Strong in organising skills: organised monthly campus lecture series on renaissance artists

Good planning skills: coordinated two 3-week workshops on diversity issues in the arts

Excellent lecturing and interviewing skills for media environment: lecture for semester long workshop on communication

EDUCATION

Master of Arts, Delhi University, Delhi, in 2004

Bachelor of Arts, Delhi University, Delhi, in 2002

WORK EXPERIENCE

August 2002 – August 2004: Programme Assistant, Supporters of Art Foundation, Delhi (Internship)

Prepared press and action alert releases

Reviewed papers published by private collectors

Created information packets for grade school students

September 2000 – October 2001: Assistant to collections manager, Institute for Art Conservation, Delhi (Internship)

Collected research of historical collections in conjunction with the national art institute conservation branch

Maintained database on endangered artworks

Copyedited press releases, in house documents, and reports

POINTS TO REMEMBER

- While looking for employment, you will need to send out messages such as resumes and application letters. Whenever you send out such employment messages, you have an opportunity to demonstrate your communication skills.
- A resume is a persuasive summary of your qualifications for employment. It is a structured, written summary of a person's education, employment background, and job qualifications.
- Certain guidelines have to be followed while planning a resume – analyse your purpose and audience, gather relevant information, tailor your resume to your audience.
- Organise your resume around your strengths: focus attention on your strongest points, select an appropriate and relevant organisational pattern, that is, make your resume chronological or functional.
- The work experience section dominates in chronological resume and is placed in the most prominent slot, immediately after the name and address, and the objective. This section includes listing your jobs sequentially in reverse order.
- A functional resume emphasises a list of skills and accomplishments, thereby focusing attention on your areas of competence.
- The contents of a resume include – name and address, career objective, work experience, education, activities and achievements, personal data, miscellaneous facts, references.
- You need to revise your resume, produce it in an appropriate from and proofread it for any errors. The perfect resume responds to the reader's needs and preferences and avoids some common faults.
- Whenever you submit your resume, accompany it with a cover, or application letter, to let readers know what you are sending, why you are sending it, and how they can benefit from reading it.
- Different types of application letters are solicited application letters and unsolicited application letters.
- Follow the AIDA approach when writing an effective application letter: attention, interest, desire and action.

Chapter

15

Interview

Learning Objectives

- To understand how today's changing workplace is affecting the hiring process
- To understand the interview process
- To discuss the various types of interviews
- To learn the 3 P's of interview
- To understand how male/female attire plays an important role in interviews
- Discuss what not to bring to an interview
- To learn the manners required for an interview
- To learn the required body language needed for an interview
- To learn how to give interviews over meals
- To understand the process of salary negotiations in interview
- To know the top 10 blunders in an interview process
- To understand why candidates fail in interviews
- Listing of commonly asked questions
- Listing of some toughest questions with tips to answer them

Many attempts to communicate are nullified by saying too much.

—Robert Greeleaf

INTRODUCTION

Anyone seeking employment nowadays realises that things are not the same as they were ten years ago. Numerous forces are changing today's workforce – globalisation, advancing technology, information overload, growing diversity and team-based organisations.

Today's employers seek people who are able and willing to adapt to diverse situations, who thrive in an ever-changing workplace, and who continue to learn throughout their careers. Moreover, companies want team players with strong work records, leaders who are versatile, and employees with diversified skills and varied job experience. In addition, they should be sensitive to intercultural differences.

An interview is a formal meeting in which a person or persons question, consult, or evaluate another person or persons. The process reveals the views, ideas and attitudes of the person being interviewed as well as the skills of the interviewer. Both the interviewer and the interviewee must be well-prepared for the interview.

An 'employment interview' is a formal meeting in which both the employer and the applicant ask questions and exchange information. Interviews have two main purposes :

1. The organisation's main objective is to find the best person available for the job by determining whether the applicant and the organisation are a best match.
2. The applicant's main objective is to find the job best suited to his or her goals and capabilities.

TYPES OF INTERVIEWS

Regardless of the type of interview you may face, a personal interview is vital because your resume, does not show whether you are lively and outgoing, or subdued and low key, able to take directions or able to take charge. Each job requires a different mix of personality traits. The interviewer's task is to find out whether you are effective for the job.

- **Structured interview:** It is generally used in the screening stage. A structural interview is controlled by the interviewer who asks a series of prepared questions in a set order, in order to gather facts. Although useful in gathering facts, the structured interview is generally regarded as a poor measure of an applicant's personal qualities.
- **Open ended interview:** It is less formal and unstructured, with a relaxed format. The interviewer poses broad, open-ended questions and encourages the applicant to talk freely. This type

of interview is good for bringing out the applicant's personality and is used to test professional judgment. However, some candidates talk and reveal too much about their personal life, which has no connection with the job they are applying for. The idea is to strike a balance between being friendly and professional.

- **Group interview:** Some organisations perform group interviews – meeting with several candidates simultaneously to see how they interact. This type of interview is useful in judging interpersonal skills.
- **Panel interview:** In a panel interview, a candidate is interviewed by several people at once. It can be quite intimidating as questions are fired at you. You should try to remain calm and establish a rapport with each member of the panel. Make eye contact with the member of the panel as you answer his/her question.
- **Stress interview:** The most unnerving type of interview is the stress interview, which is set up to see how well a candidate handles stressful situations. This type of interview deliberately puts the applicant under stress. Usually the stress is psychological by asking pointed questions designed to unsettle or irk you. You might be subjected to long periods of silence, criticisms of your appearance, deliberate interruptions, and abrupt or even hostile reactions by the interviewer.
- **Phone interview:** Try to schedule phone interviews from home, not work, and for a time when things will be quiet. If a company wants to interview you on the spot, accept only if the timing is good. To prepare for a phone interview.
    1. Tape yourself so that you can make any adjustments in pronunciation and voice qualities.
    2. Practice short answers to questions. After giving a short answer in the interview, say, 'Would you like more information?' Without a visual channel, you cannot see the body language that tells you someone else wants to speak.
    3. Keep a copy of your resume and the job description near the phone.
    4. Ask the interviewer to spell his or her name, get the title, phone number, mailing address and e-mail address. You may need this information later on.
    5. Smile when you talk to put more energy in your voice.

- **Situational interview:** In these types of interviews, candidates must explain how they would handle a specific set of circumstances. The interviewer describes a situation and asks, "How would you handle this?" Many companies have learnt that there is no correlation between how well people answer questions in a traditional interview and how well they perform on the job.
- **Behavioural interview:** These types of interviews ask the applicant to describe actual behaviours, rather than plans or general principles. Thus, instead of asking, "How would you motivate people?" The interviewer might ask, "Tell me what happened the last time you wanted to get other people to do something".

  Some common behavioural interview questions are given below. Describe a situation in which you
  - created an opportunity for yourself in a job or volunteer position
  - used writing to achieve your goal
  - went beyond the call of duty to get a job done
  - communicated successfully with someone you disliked
  - had to make a decision quickly
  - overcame a major obstacle
  - took a project from start to finish
  - were unable to complete a project on time
  - used good judgment and logic in solving a problem
  - worked under a tight deadline
  - worked with a tough boss
  - handled a difficult situation with a co-worker
  - made an unpopular decision
  - gave a presentation
  - worked with someone who was not doing his or her share of work
- **Video interview:** This type of interview is becoming popular because it tries to cut travel costs. Many large companies use videoconferencing systems to hire middle management candidates or interview new recruits at universities. The

preparation for this type of interview varies slightly in the following ways :

- Arrive early enough to get used to the equipment and setting.
- During the interview, speak clearly, but not more slowly than normal.
- Sit straight.
- Look up but not down.
- Smile when you talk to put more energy in your voice.

3 P'S OF INTERVIEW

Interviews, like anything else in life, take practice to perfect. The job market is highly competitive so you should always maintain a high standard of professionalism. This is guaranteed to impress your potential employer, as it will show focus and maturity.

Professionalism is – Presentation, Punctuality and Preparation.

Presentation: Presentation is not just the clothes you wear, but your general presentation during the interview. Dress for success; formal attire is the best option. Look the part and you will be more likely to get it. Body language such as eye contact and how you greet your interviewer are important. Shaking hands is a sign of confidence and respect so is making regular eye contact. Always be polite not just during the interview but to any one you may have contact with in the office or work environment.

Punctuality: Being on time is essential to a successful interview. Give yourself plenty of time to get to your destination, map out a route if you are unsure in any way. Being early gives you time to relax and prepare yourself. If you are going to be late or unable to attend for any unforeseeable reason call ahead and let them know. This will show them that you are serious and that you take your commitments seriously.

Preparation: Get to know the company you are hoping to work for. A little background information can go a long way. You should research the company well before applying to it. You must be prepared to discuss the industry, the company's relative size within that industry and show that you know who the major players and competitors are.

HOW TO DRESS

Does it really make a difference how you dress for an interview? In many cases, it does.

In the conservative business climate, appearances do matter. In other environments it is not as important. However, it does make sense to dress your best for the interview, regardless of the dress code at the organisation. If you are in doubt about how to dress, it is best to err on the side of conservatism. It is much better to be overdressed than underdressed (or undressed!). A big part of another person's perception of you is based on how you look.

Women's Interview Attire

- Solid colour, conservative suit
- Coordinated blouse
- Moderate shoes
- Limited jewellery
- Neat, professional hairstyle
- Sparse make-up and perfume
- Manicured nails
- Portfolio or briefcase

Men's Interview Attire

- Solid colour, conservative suit
- White long sleeved shirt
- Conservative tie
- Dark socks, professional shoes
- Very limited jewellery
- Neat, professional hairstyle
- Go easy on the aftershave
- Neatly trimmed nails
- Portfolio or briefcase

What not to Bring to the Interview

- Gum
- Cell phone
- I pod
- Coffee or soda
- If you have lots of piercing, leave some of your rings at home (earrings only, is a good rule)

Interview Attire Tips

- Before you even think about going for an interview, make sure you have appropriate interview attire and everything fits correctly.
- Get your clothes ready the night before, so you do not have to spend time getting them ready on the day of the interview.

- If your clothes are dry-clean only, take them to the cleaners after an interview, so they are ready for next time.
- Polish your shoes.
- Bring a breath mint and use it before you enter the building.

MANNERS FOR A JOB INTERVIEW

Interviews are stressful events almost for everyone on the face of this earth. Many employers employ different methodologies to analyse the ability of handling stress of the potential employees. It may even include dining outside or taking you for a ride. However, in simple cases, every job interview demands some general and basic etiquette. This guide helps you in exploring some of them.

Be on time: Time management is the first step for showing good manners in many events. It is crucially important for a job interview. If you are late for the interview, it may leave a negative impression on the employer. He has the right to assume that you will be late during reporting time as well.

Dress professionally: Your dress and the way you wear it can make an ever-lasting impression. If you wear a clean, well-pressed dress, it may imply that you are taking the interview seriously and also as to the job.

Be prepared: Do not forget to carry extra copies of your resume with you. Be up-to-date as far as possible about the potential employer. It will help you to answer the critical questions regarding the organisation, post and job responsibilities.

Work extra hard on your body language: Smile costs nothing, but offers a good return. This is always true. So maintain a pleasant smile and a good posture even if you are feeling rather nervous. It will benefit you a lot during the interview.

Be friendly, but in limit: Like exploring your talent and capabilities, the interviewer must also focus on those personality traits that are significant in defining your ability to suit the organisation's culture. But you should always remember that the employer does not need to hear your entire life story for you to get involved in the organisation. So, it is important to maintain a professional level during the conversation.

Thank the interviewer: A written or e-mailed note thanking the interviewer is not, as yet, a very common occurence, however, it may accelerate the tipping of the job scale in your favour if there is hard competition for the position you have applied for.

BODY LANGUAGE FOR INTERVIEW

Never underestimate the importance of body language during a job interview. Make sure you are sending all the right messages.

Start strong: The interview starts the moment you step into the interview because your body language clearly depicts your mental attitude. A person walking head down, with stooping shoulders, and heavy steps gives the impression of a depressed/dejected/non-confident person, whereas a person with a straight head, erect shoulders, fast steps and straight posture gives the impression of a confident and warm person. Our reaction to stressful mental and emotional situations clearly reflects in the position of our head and neck.

Handshake: Shake hands only if the interviewer offers his/her hand. The handshake too conveys a lot about the personality of a person and his attitude towards the other person. All of us have experienced various types of handshakes. Recollect how you felt when someone just placed his lifeless hand in your hand in a loose grip. A weak, limp, dead fish handshake gives the impression of a disinterested and cold person; it also signifies lack of enthusiasm. A strong, well-gripped handshake gives the impression of a warm, friendly and enthusiastic person. Make the handshake strong and firm, pumping hands once or twice, and then release. A weak handshake as well as bone crushers can both leave a negative impression. Also make sure that your hand is free as you offer it to the interviewer.

Always remember that the handshake is an integral part of one's personality and modifying your handshake can improve your initial image. Practice a strong and well-gripped handshake.

The interviewer will usually offer you a chair. If not, go to the chair across from him/her and ask if it is alright to sit. Use the entire chair. If you are sitting on the edge, you are going to look nervous and uncomfortable.

Eye movements: Eyes speak more than words and convey a lot of our feelings. When we are not interested in listening to something, we tend to break eye contact or look somewhere else. Shutting the eyes for a brief period or blinking them at more than the normal pace is an indication of our disbelief and disinterest in the subject under discussion. It is also an escapist reaction, indicating a desire to avoid discussing the matter.

When you blink/flicker your eyelids too fast, it indicates nervousness. Short eye contacts which are frequently broken while talking indicate that the person is shy or is telling a lie (if supported by other gestures). The best tactic for an interviewee is to practice continuous eye contact and avoid looking anywhere else, or breaking eye contact erratically. It may make you a little uncomfortable if you are a bit shy (or telling a lie). In such a situation, the best practice is to look just above the eyes of the interviewer, near the forehead (above the nose) while speaking.

Be an active listener: Forget everything else and focus your entire attention on the interviewer. Leaning forward, nodding and smiling when appropriate are forms of effective body language. Not only you will look interested, but it will probably be easier to pay attention.

If you are being interviewed by a group of people, talk directly to the person that is asking the question. Once you have fully answered to that individual, then look at the other interviewers. You should not ignore any of the people who are interviewing, but you should give priority to the person who is asking the question.

Gestures: Expressing yourself with your hands portrays energy and passion. But don't over do it as it will overwhelm the interviewer. Avoid jiggling legs and keep your feet flat on the floor (or at most, cross your ankles). This not only cuts down on restless legs, but helps you sit straighter. Never cross your legs in an interview. It gives the impression of being non-receptive to others ideas and feelings. Do not play with your hair. Do not glance at your watch every now and then and stop playing with your jewellery. In short, fidgeting makes you look nervous and distracted.

Finish strong: Finish the interview the way you started it – with energy and confidence (even if the interview went bad!). Shake hands while you thank the interviewer for the opportunity, and walk away with your shoulders back and head high. You never know what is going to happen and can never regret leaving a good impression.

The best way to show positive body language at an interview is to be natural, comfortable and confident. Always remember that no matter what happens, an interview is an opportunity to learn. You can evaluate yourself at the end, and ask yourself what you did right and wrong, and how you could improve.

INTERVIEW OVER MEALS

Employers may want to see how you conduct yourself over a meal, particularly if the job requires a certain standard of conduct with clients. On a practical level, interviews that last for several hours may extend through mealtimes, so the interviewer acts as the host.

Who should sit down first?

You should wait for your interviewer/host to ask you to sit down before taking your seat. If he/she does not ask you to sit, wait for him/ her to be seated, then sit.

Which fork is for what?

Use your cutlery from the outside in. so if you have two forks, the outside fork is for salad and the fork closest to the plate is for your main course. The cutlery will be removed as you finish each course. There may be a third fork outside the salad fork for appetizers. Usually no more than three utensils are placed on each side of the place setting. If a fourth utensil is needed, it is placed above the plate and is usually for dessert.

What do I do with my napkin?

As soon as everyone is seated, unfold your napkin and place it across your lap, folded, with the fold towards you. If you need to leave the table, place the napkin on your chair, folded loosely (never wadded). Only after the meal is over, you should place your napkin on the table to the left side of your plate.

How do you wipe your mouth with the napkin? Is it considered poor etiquette to wipe one's mouth with the napkin?

It is poor etiquette NOT to use your napkin. The purpose of the napkin is to keep food off your face. Use it frequently to discreetly wipe (no ear to ear swiping please!) your mouth. Replace the napkin on your lap loosely folded, not wadded and not stuffed between your legs.

When is it okay to begin drinking and eating? Do I wait until the host/hostess starts eating his/her meal?

It is appropriate to sip your water after everyone is seated and after you have placed your napkin in your lap. For other beverages and foods, wait until everyone has been served, and do not eat until your host/hostess has begun; when your host picks up his/her fork, this is an indicator that you may also do so.

Do I have a drink if I am offered one?

Try and avoid alcohol if it is an official meeting. At most, one glass of wine is acceptable. You want to remain sharp and responsive.

What should be ordered for dinner?

Simple foods that are easily eaten with a fork and knife should be ordered. Avoid spaghetti and other things with red sauce, huge sandwiches, and greasy hand-held items like pizza. Sometimes you may not have a choice.

Is it best to avoid ordering a food if you cannot pronounce its name?

No. if you like it, ask the server to describe the food, and point it on the menu.

How does one eat and answer questions at the same time?

By taking very small bites, so that you can eat and swallow before speaking. Never speak with food in your mouth. You may not have much time to eat if you are being asked a lot of questions; remember that the main point of the meal is to interact and eating is secondary. Don't eat too quickly and don't attempt to hurriedly scarf down all your food. A large, hurriedly eaten meal can make you drowsy and uncomfortable.

How should soup be consumed?

Dip your spoon away from yourself to fill it with soup. Rest your spoon periodically. When a service plate under the soup bowl is provided, always place your spoon on the service plate behind the bowl. If no service plate is provided, rest your spoon in the soup bowl only. Used utensils are never placed on the table. Sip quietly.

Should one go out of one's way to use utensils when eating finger food?

When in doubt, eat with a utensil rather than with your fingers, even foods like French fries that you may eat by hand at home. If something is served on plate, you should use utensils! Chicken, or any other meat with a bone, is not a finger food, you should use the fork and knife.

NEGOTIATING SALARY

Negotiating your salary is a very important part of the job search process. These negotiations can set the tone for your work life and experience with an employer. It is best to wait until after you receive a job offer, to start talking about compensation. Since negotiating is a two-way street, try to achieve a win-win situation.

Know what you want and prioritise what's most important to you in your next role –money, more responsibility, work/life balance, a shorter commute, corporate culture –before you begin interviewing.

Once you know what you *should* be earning, how do you go about getting it? Start by being very patient. When being interviewed for a new position, do your best not to bring up compensation until the employer makes you an offer. If you're asked what your salary requirements are, say that they are open based upon the position and the overall compensation package. Or tell the employer you would like to know more about the responsibilities and the challenges of the job prior to discussing salary. Another option is to give the employer a salary range based upon the salary research you have done up front. Once you have received the offer you do not need to accept (or reject) it right away. A simple 'I need to think it over' can get you an increase in the original offer.

Negotiating a Raise

If you are currently employed and want a raise, start by being prepared. Gather your salary survey information, recent performance appraisals that document the job you are doing, and any other relevant information. Be aware of company policy regarding compensation. Some employers are limited by budget constraints and can only give raises at certain times of the year, regardless of the circumstances. Have a clear idea of what you want. Determine the salary range you are looking for, and justification for the increase, and have both ready to review with your supervisor. Be flexible. Only when you are fully prepared, ask your supervisor for a meeting to discuss salary. Present your request, supported by documentation, calmly and rationally. Don't ask for an immediate answer. Your boss is most likely going to have to discuss it with Human Resources and/or other company managers.

Despite your best efforts, there may simply not be enough money in the budget to increase your salary or compensation package offer. The company may also not want to create inequities by paying one person more than others in a similar position. In that case, you can at least know you tried. Plus, if this is a job you really think that you are going to love, consider whether the company culture, the benefits, and the job itself are worth it – regardless of the salary.

BASIC ISSUES IN NEGOTIATING THE JOB OFFER

Unless some of the following issues were discussed in the interviews, you have every right to be clear on issues such as the following, depending on the level at which you enter the company.

1. Your total compensation package:

(a) **Cash issues:** You need to be clear about your starting base pay and salary range of position, bonus for signing (if any) and how it will be paid, stock options (if any) or profit sharing or other payments, salary review schedule.

(b) **Fringe or other benefits issues:** These include vacation payments length of vacations; car and auto expenses; club memberships; health care issues: long-term disability, accident insurance, dental plan, death benefits, sick leave, health insurance, and persons covered by insurance; discounts on purchase of employer products; life insurance; recreation programmes.

2. Your position: Extent of your authority, members of your staff, statement of your precise responsibilities, individual to whom you will report, range of your budget, title of the position.

3. Your work environment: What is the precise location of my job? What are the expected hours of work during the day and week? What are the resources, supplies and facilities? What is the work culture of the company?

4. Your beginning/ending work benefits: Starting date of the new position; housing assistance: disposal of former residence and acquiring another; relocating assistance from current to new location: travel, moving charges (highly important when working with an employer overseas).

It is preferable to carry out your negotiations orally rather than in writing. Doing so gives you the power of both oral and non-verbal persuasion to accompany your credentials. There is no set formula for negotiating successfully – just be fair, listen to the other side, come prepared for arguments for your position. Have your facts straight.

Suggested Tips for Negotiating a Salary

- Know the salary you can reasonably accept and expect for the type of position you seek in comparison with your experience, education, and the industry wage standards.
- Try and find out the salary range for the position before the interview. Contacting the interviewer's secretary, the personnel office, or a networking contact that works in the company may be helpful.
- It is not usually recommended to accept an offer on the spot. Express your appreciation and strong interest in the job. Request at least 24 hours to consider it, even when saying 'Yes'. Ask any questions you need clarified.
- Assess the job offer in terms of your needs, benefits, and long-term career and life goals. Talk it over with someone you respect. Make a list of the pros and cons of the job offer.
- Consider if the job description is clear. Note your reporting relationships, authority, and advancement potential. Keep asking questions until you understand everything clearly. Careful thought and consideration will only gain you respect.
- If you want the job, make it clear that it is the job you want. If you are uncertain, state there are some items you would like to discuss before you can accept the job. Suggest meeting further to talk about the offer.
- Begin the negotiation with reasonable requests. Those requests could include more money, employee benefits, training, more

vacation time, a flexible schedule, stock options, company car, on-site daycare, parking privileges, etc.

- Negotiations should never become emotional or hostile. Use your value, skills, experience, and education to negotiate. Do not use your need for the job to negotiate.
- Listen carefully. If the offer is less than you expected, let them know that, but state you are still interested in the position if they want to reconsider their offer. Don't assume the first offer to be fixed. Even if the interviewer tells you it is, it rarely is.
- Avoid naming a specific salary. Never say you cannot accept less, always say, 'I would find it difficult to accept the offer.'
- If the same figure is offered a couple of days later, it probably is the last offer. In that case, you can ask for a salary review in six months to evaluate your performance and value, or you can turn the job down, asking that they keep you in mind for future openings paying more money.
- Even when saying 'no', leave the door open to negotiation. (Do not use this to negotiate a higher wage. When you say 'no', be ready to lose the job forever.)
- When you reach an agreement, request the agreement in writing.

What to do if you cannot Compromise on Compensation

- Let the interviewers know that although you are disappointed, you are still interested in working for the employer.
- Be sure to thank them for their time and interest. Re-emphasise the fact that if future openings occur, you would be interested.
- Find out if there are, or might be, other openings they could suggest or other persons you could contact.
- Many times the person selected ends up turning the job down or does not work out. Keep the communication line open, positive, and professional. This keeps your name in their mind for the next opening or future opportunities.
- Ask if you could contact them every three or four months to find out about future job openings.
- Stay positive. Congratulate yourself. You did get the interview, which means the employer was interested in you. Use positive self-talk.
- Learn from the experience. Ask for feedback from the interviewer on what you could improve or do differently.

- Keep trying. This is not the time to stop. Forge ahead. Act to stay in control of your job search.
- Remember the salesperson's motto: 'No' is another step closer to 'Yes'.
- Do not despair. Getting turned down happens to all of us at some point in our lives.

TOP 10 INTERVIEW BLUNDERS

Here is a selection of blunders, mistakes and errors a candidate for employment can make :

1. **Not prepared well:** Not being able to answer the question 'What do you know about this company?' might just end your quest for employment, at least with this employer. Background information including company history, locations, divisions, and a mission statement are available in the 'About Us' section on most company websites. Review it ahead of time, then print it out and read it over just before your interview to refresh your memory.
2. **Dressing inappropriately:** "Dressing inappropriately is bleenar when going for an interview". You will certainly want to wear a suit if you are interviewing for a professional position. If you are not sure what to wear, visit the organisation and watch employees coming in and out of the office to see what they are wearing.
3. **Poor communication skills:** It is important to communicate well with everyone you meet in your search for employment. It is, however, most important to positively connect with the person who might hire you. Shake hands, make eye contact, exude confidence, engage the person you are speaking with, and you will let the interviewer know that you are an excellent candidate for this position – before you even answer an interview question.
4. **Too much communication:** Leave the phone behind or at least turn it off before you enter the building. Same goes for coffee, food and anything else other than you, your resume, your job application, and your list of references. They do not belong at an interview.
5. **Talking too much:** There is nothing much worse than interviewing someone who goes on and on and on... The interviewer really does not need to know your whole life story.

Keep your answers succinct, to-the-point and focused, and do not ramble – simply answer the question.

6. **Not talking enough:** It's really hard to communicate with someone who answers a question with a word or two. So, even though you should not talk too much, you do want to be responsive and fully answer the question as best as you can.
7. **Being fuzzy about facts:** Even if you have submitted a resume when you applied for the job, you may also be asked to fill out a job application. Make sure you know the information you will need to complete an application including dates of prior employment, graduation dates, and employer contact information.
8. **Giving the wrong answer:** Make sure you listen to the question and take a moment to gather your thoughts before you respond. In one instance, the interviewer had described a sales and marketing position to the candidate in detail. She emphasised that cold calling and prospecting were the most important skills and experiences needed for the position. The candidate responded to the question about what she did or did not like to do in sales, with these words: 'I hate to do cold calling and prospecting, and I am not good at it'. That response ensured that she would not get the job!
9. **Badmouthing past employers:** Your last boss was an idiot? Everyone in the company was a jerk? You hated your job and could not wait to leave? Even if it's true do not say so. It leaves a bad impression on the interviewer when he/she hears someone ranting and raving about the last company they worked for. Often it is a smaller world than you think and you do not know who your interviewer might know, including that boss who is an idiot... You also do not want the interviewer to think that you might speak that way about his or her company if you leave on terms that are not the best.
10. **Forgeting to follow up:** Afraid you did not make the best impression? Either way, be sure to follow up with a thank you note showing your interest in the position and the company.

A RECAP OF WHAT TO DO/NOT TO DO WHILE PREPARING FOR AN INTERVIEW

- **Why do candidates fail in an interview? Because of**
  - poor grooming

- discourteous and ungraceful body language
- poor manners
- poor diction
- vague responses
- unappealing resume
- monetary benefits-centric approach
- lack of punctuality
- poor waiting hall behaviour

❑ **Some behavioural 'unfavourable' aspects: Here is a list.**

- Lack of personal or career goals
- Lack of enthusiasm and confidence
- Not owning up responsibility for mistakes
- Self-justification, aggressiveness
- Lack of emotional maturity
- Negative and cynical attitude
- Over-reacting to questions
- Lacking sense of humor
- Complaining about various things and previous employers

❑ **White Preparing for an interview, look for**

- The company's main products and services and likely new products and services
- Its key markets, its position in the market and between major competitors
- Its financial position / profit / turnover
- Its history, reputation and achievements
- Arrange all the papers required in a folder: Resume / CV, call letters, degree certificates, mark lists, NSS, NCC, sports / games certificates, experience certificates, references.

❑ **On the previous day**

- confirm the venue of the interview, distance, and mode of transport
- locate the venue
- relax, have a good sleep, visualise and pray

❑ **On the interview day**

- reach the venue at least 45 minutes ahead of the interview
- get familiar with the ambience
- don't carry too much baggage
- report to the authority concerned

- **Waiting hall behaviour**
  - Maintain decorum
  - Mingle with others politely
  - Avoid smoking, chewing, flirting, gossiping, defamatory comments
  - Greet others present
  - Switch off the mobile
  - Relax

COMMON INTERVIEW QUESTIONS

Questions about college

- What courses in college did you like the most? Least? Why?
- Do you think your extra curricular activities in college were worth the time you spent on them? Why, or why not?
- Which of your college years was toughest? Why?
- Do you feel you did the best academic work you are capable of?

Questions about employers and jobs

- What jobs have you held? Why did you leave?
- Why did you choose your particular field of work?
- What are the disadvantages of your chosen field?
- What do you think about how this industry operates today?

Questions about personal attitudes and preferences

- Do you prefer to work in any specific geographic location? If so, why?
- How much money do you hope to be earning in 5 years? In 10 years?
- What do you think determines a person's progress in an organisation?
- What personal characteristics do you feel are necessary for success in your chosen field?
- Tell me a story.
- Do you like to travel?
- Do you think grades should be considered by employers? Why, or why not?

Questions about work habits

- Do you prefer working with others or by yourself?
- What type of boss do you prefer?

- Have you ever had any difficulty getting along with your colleagues or supervisors? With instructors? With other students?
- How do you feel about overtime work?
- What have you performed that demonstrates initiative and willingness to work?

HOW TO ANSWER SOME TOUGH QUESTIONS?

The answers to challenging interview questions can reveal a lot about the candidate. You can expect to face several such questions during every interview. If you are prepared with thoughtful answers, you are bound to make a good impression.

Tell me something about yourself.

This is where most applicants fail. They start rattling about their family and personal lives in which the interviewer has no interest. Don't launch into an autobiography. Instead, state the things about yourself that you want the interviewer to know. Explain how your skills can contribute to the job and the organisation. This is a great chance to sell yourself.

Why should we employ you?

Emphasise your academic strengths, and enthusiasm for the company. Tailor your specific skills to the employer's needs and give examples of how you can learn and become productive quickly. Cite past activities to prove you can work with others as part of a team.

If we hire you, what changes will you make?

No one can know what to change in a position before settling in and learning about the job and company operations. State that you would take a good hard look at everything the company is doing before making recommendations.

What was the toughest decision you ever had to make?

Be prepared with a good example, explaining why the decision was difficult and how you decided.

Why do you want to work for this organisation?

Show that you have done your homework, and cite some things going on in the company currently which appeal to you the most.

What are your greatest strengths?

Employers ask this question to give you a chance to sell yourself. Answer sincerely by summarising your strong points – 'I am good at working with people'. 'I am willing to make decisions'. 'I am good at solving problems'. Be ready to illustrate each with a specific example of something you have done.

What are your greatest weaknesses?

Use a work-related negative, even if something in your personal life is your greatest weakness. Describe a weakness so that it sounds like a virtue. Reveal something about yourself which works to an employer's advantage. For example, you can say that you drive yourself too hard, but it helps when you have to meet some deadlines.

What did not you like about the previous jobs you have held?

Do not attempt at mud slinging your previous organisation and employers. It will create a bad impression on the interviewer. No organisation wants a cribbing employee. Rather, state tactfully what you did not like (without making any pointed references to the employers) and discuss what the experience taught you.

How do you spend your leisure time?

Rather than focusing on one activity, mention a cross-section of interests – active and quiet, social and solitary.

Where do you want to be five years from now?

Employers pose this question to test whether you are merely using this job as a stopover until something better comes along; or whether you have given thought to your long term goals. Saying that you will be the CEO of a company is unrealistic, so your answer should reflect your long-term goals and the company's advancement opportunities.

What are your salary expectations?

The best time to discuss salary and benefits is after you have the job offer. Try to delay discussing salary early in the interview process. Try this response – 'I am sure your firm can pay me what I am worth'. Then you can ask for pay ranges. If the interviewer demands a response, give a range: 'I would expect to make between ....and .....' As you say this, watch the interviewer. If he or she has a blank look (which is generally used to hide dismay), you may have asked for much more than the company was planning to offer.

Quickly continue, 'Depending of course on fringe benefits and how quickly could I be promoted. However, salary is not the most important criterion for me in choosing a job. I am interested in going somewhere where I can get good experience and use my talents to make a contribution.'

The best way to get more money is to convince the employer that you are worth it.

Do you have any questions about the organisation or the job?

Employers like candidates who are interested in the organisation. Convey your interest and enthusiasm. Moreover, it also gives you a chance to cover things that the interviewer has not brought up. Don't focus on salary and fringe benefits.

Be sure that your answers are sincere, truthful and positive. Take a moment to compose your thoughts before responding, so that your answers are to the point.

POINTS TO REMEMBER

- Numerous forces are changing today's workforce – globalisation, advancing technology, information overload, growing diversity and team-based organisations.
- An employment interview is a formal meeting in which both the employer and the applicant ask questions and exchange information.
- There are various types of interview – structured, open-ended, group, panel, stress, phone, situational, behavioural, and video interview.
- In the conservative business climate, appearances do matter. However, it does make sense to dress your best for the interview, regardless of the dress code at the organisation. There are certain guidelines to be followed by men and women when it comes to dressing for an interview.
- Every job interview demands some general manners and etiquettes.
- Never underestimate the importance of body language during a job interview. Make sure you are sending all the right messages.
- Employers may want to see how you conduct yourself, particularly if the job requires a certain standard of conduct with clients. On a practical level, interviews that last for several hours may extend through mealtimes, so the employer acts as the host.
- Negotiating your salary is a very important part of the job search process. These negotiations can set the tone for your work life and experience with an employer.

Chapter

16

Case-Study Analysis

Learning Objectives

- To know the nature and types of case studies
- To understand the process of case analysis
- To identify major problems/questions involved in the case study
- To consider alternative solutions/answers to the questions
- To choose the best solution

Communication works for those who work at it.

—John Powell

CASE – STUDY

A case is a written account of real or simulated managerial problems, dilemmas and situations calling for solutions. It develops skills in diagnosing situations, defining problems, analysing the sources and constraints of problems, developing alternative courses of action, and deciding on a particular course of action.

The idea behind case study is that students are more likely to retain and use concepts through practical case studies than through lectures or note-taking. Cases present a general and useful way of thinking about, analysing and solving actual business problems. It helps in developing skills necessary for becoming an effective manager.

TYPES OF CASES

1. **The Formal Case:** It describes a simulated or real-life situation faced by management. It may deal with a specific problem experienced by one company or by an industry as a whole. The problem and events are not good or bad, and a single best solution may or may not exist.

   The case might focus on issues such as: Should a franchise fast food chain add a new food product? Should a company move from one location to another? Should a company diversify, merge or acquire? What marketing strategies should be applied in a particular situation?

2 **The Case Story:** It is usually written like a news story, as a history of a decision made by the management. The outcome and an analysis of the decision are presented and little excess information is given. In it, the management's solution to the problem may not be the best. This type of case focuses on issues such as: marketing processes, sales method, company events, product failures and human behaviour.

3. **The Critical incident:** While the formal case often involves long-term, strategic decisions, the critical incident case asks – 'What should we do NOW?' and involves more immediate issues. This type of case usually gives little background information. The opening paragraph of this type of case often throws you in the middle of a dilemma.

APPLYING THE SIX-STEP CASE ANALYSIS PROCESS

Step 1: Study the case

Gain familiarity with the basic details of the case. Seek to determine the who, what, where, when, where and how. In detail identify the people, organisation, activities and context of the situation.

Step 2: Identify the problem and write a problem statement

It is rightly said that a problem well-defined is half-solved. Defining a problem is not simple, but once done, the definition logically leads the person doing the analysis towards the possible solutions. List the problems and their symptoms and try to distinguish between the two. For example, strikes in an organisation can be viewed as a problem. Rather they are the symptoms of something being wrong in the organisation, its work culture, goals and objectives.

Problems are barriers that threaten to block an organisation or person from achieving important goals.

A good problem statement should be descriptive, zeroing in on the key issue that must be addressed. It should not rehearse the case in detail.

Step 3: Analyse the facts and assumptions

State relevant facts and establish logical links with them. Always remember that facts are not opinions.

If you have made any assumptions while analysing, state them clearly. Always look for assumptions that are reasonable and realistic. Moreover, while searching for assumptions, remember to distinguish between causes and effects, which are often related. For example, an organisation is losing money (effect). One reason (cause) is that customers are no longer buying the company's product (effect). Investigations show that the product is of poor quality (cause). The poor quality of the product (effect) is a direct result of the company not spending money on R & D to update the product (cause). Further researching reveals that the top management had made a decision to cut the budget (effect) because of cost cutting measures (cause).

Step 4: List possible alternative solutions

For every problem, there are a host of solutions. Do not be limited to minimal alternatives, which seem to easily arise out of the case. As you identify solutions, consider the criteria that must be met in order to accomplish each solution. List advantages and disadvantages of each. Weighing them against each other will logically guide to the best solution.

Do not pre-determine the best solution at this juncture.

Step 5: Select the best solution

After analysing the case in depth, you should be able to select the best solution. The best solution should always directly address the problem which you have left isolated in Step 2. In stating your solution, state how it will solve the problem. The points and recommendations must be short and concise. Use logic and reasoning from case analysis to defend your selection.

Step 6: Develop a plan of action to carry out the best solution

Develop an action plan for carrying out the solution. Your plan should clearly state the specific steps involved. List the advantages and disadvantages, costs and benefits of your solution. Consider the possibility of success, the risks involved, and what will happen if failure occurs, thereby making room for a backup plan.

DO' S OF CASE ANALYSIS

1. Always remember and accept the fact that much of the material in the case is useless to your investigation.
2. Just as there is no one managerial style, there is no one case analysis style.
3. Follow a logical, clear and consistent path through the case analysis.
4. Distinguish between facts and inferences. Strive to base your analysis more on facts rather than assumptions and suppositions.
5. Take a stand in your analysis and support it.

DONT'S OF CASE ANALYSIS

1. Don't expect a right conclusion to be available after the case is analysed.
2. Lack of information is common in all cases, so don't ask for more information.
3. Don't be short-sighted in deciding the best solution for the problem in the case. Develop alternatives and narrow them down to the best solution by weighing their pros and cons.
4. You don't have to solve all the problems in the case. There are major and minor problems in every case. Tackle the major and critical issues. Develop alternative solutions to one problem at a time and then move on to the next problem.

POINTS TO REMEMBER

- A case is a written account of real or simulated managerial problems, dilemmas and situations calling for solutions.
- The different types of cases are: formal case, case story, critical incident.
- Apply the six-step case analysis process: study the case; identify the problem and write a problem statement; analyse the facts and assumptions; list possible alternative solutions; select the best solution; and develop a plan of action to carry out the best solution.
- Certain guidelines have to be kept in mind while analysing a case study.

INDEX

V

W

Y